TEACHING YOUNG CHILDREN WITH AUTISM

Clarissa Willis

Featherstone

Published 2011 by Featherstone Education
Bloomsbury Publishing Plc
50 Bedford Square
London
WC1B 3DP

First published in 2006 by Gryphon House Inc
PO Box 207, Beltsville, MD 20704
www.ghbooks.com

ISBN 978-1-4081-3972-1

Text © Clarissa Willis
Photographs © Michael Talley
Illlustrations © Marie Ferrante Doyle
Sign language illustrations by Rodney Paull
Design by Bob Vickers
Cover photographs © Shutterstock

A CIP record for this publication is available from the British Library.

Printed in Great Britain by Martins the Printers, Berwick-upon-Tweed.

This book is produced using paper that is made from wood grown in
managed, sustainable forests. It is natural, renewable and recyclable.
The logging and manufacturing processes conform to the environmental
regulations of the country of origin.

To see our full range of titles
visit www.acblack.com

Contents

Introduction   5

Chapter 1: **Putting all the pieces together**   7

How is autism defined?   7
Why is it called Autism Spectrum Disorder?   9
Autism – the myths   10
Words, words, words – why is there so much autism-related jargon?   11
What are the major types of Autism Spectrum Disorder?   12
When and how is autism diagnosed?   14
What do I need to know about children with autism?   14
Key terms   16

Chapter 2: **From hand flapping to obsession with routines**   17

What can I expect a pre-school child with autism to do?   17
How do I assess a child with autism?   27
The learning characteristics of children with autism summarised   29
Key terms   30

Chapter 3: **Planning for success**   31

I know children with autism learn differently, but what can I do about it?   31
How do I arrange an early years environment for success?   32
How do I set up predictable routines for a child with autism that will not be
boring for other children?   33
What can I do to make all children feel part of the group?   34
Strategies to help children make a positive start   36–48
Key terms   49

Chapter 4: **Learning self-help skills**   50

What are self-help skills?   50
Why are self-help skills important?   51
How do I teach every day tasks?   51
What do I do first, before teaching a new skill?   53
How does this all fit together?   55
Strategies to help children learn self-help skills   57–67
Key terms   68

Chapter 5: **Misbehaviour or missed communication**   69

How will I ever understand the unusual behaviours of children with autism?   69
Some strategies for dealing with challenging behaviours   70
What is meant by form and function?   70
How can I determine the function or reason for a child's behaviour?   71
How do I know what procedure to use?   73
Strategies to help children manage behaviour   75–80
Key terms   81

Chapter 6: **Signs, symbols and language**   82

What exactly is communication?   82
How does communication differ in children with autism in the early years?   82
What do we mean by communication that is not meaningful?   83
How can non-functional communication be functional for the child?   83
What exactly is echolalia?   84
Why do children with autism have so much trouble communicating?   85
What is intentional communication?   86
How do I start helping a child communicate?   87
How do I set appropriate goals for communication?   90
Should I stop trying to make her talk and use an alternative form of communication?   92
When and how is the best way to use sign language?   93
How can a child with autism use pictures to communicate?   94
What about electronic communication devices?   95
Strategies to help children communicate   97–105
Key terms   106

Chapter 7: **Inside their own worlds**   107

How does the play of children with autism differ from their peers?   107
What can I do to encourage children to play?   109
How do I use what I have observed?   109
How do I select an appropriate peer buddy?   111
How do I begin to teach this process?   111
Ideas and activities for encouraging children to play   112
General suggestions for teaching play strategies   113
Strategies to help children with autism when they play   114–124
Key terms   125

Chapter 8: **Building social skills**   126

Why are social skills important?   126
What are the stages of social development?   126
Which social skills should be learned first?   127
How do I teach social skills to a child with autism?   129
Strategies to help children develop social skills   133–143
Key terms   143

Chapter 9: **Lights! Camera! Action!**   144

What exactly is sensory integration?   144
What do we mean by a sensory integration disorder?   145
Do you mean that children with autism see or hear differently?   145
How will I know if a child has a sensory integration disorder?   146
What can I do to help a child with sensory integration disorder?   149
What can I do to make sure that a child with autism does not go into sensory overload?   149
Strategies to help children who have sensory integration disorder   151–157
Key terms   158

Chapter 10: **We're all in this together!**   159

What can I do to understand a family's perspective?   159
What is the cycle of grief and loss?   161
How do I let parents know I need their help?   162
What can I do to make family interactions positive?   163
Key terms   164

Glossary of terms   165–169
Index   170–175

Introduction

While the other children play at activities in the early years setting, Gina looks out of the window as if she is watching a bird flying across the sky. She stands at the window for 30 minutes, silently wringing her hands, smiling and humming to herself. During periods of transition, Graham flaps his hands repeatedly and rocks back and forth. He can tell you all the words to his favourite song, but when asked his name, he looks away.

It is lunch time and everyone sits down at the table. Today will be a challenge, because Darren only eats things that are white and cannot tolerate noise or bright light.

All the children at the pre-school are going on a trip to the local shops. They will buy food and then prepare their own snacks. While most children look forward to a trip to the shops, for Janine, it is a nightmare of sounds, smells and textures that overload her system and cause her to fall to the ground screaming.

Marcus tolerates other people. In fact, sometimes he will hug his parents when they ask. He can already count to 20, even though he is only four, and his favourite activities are watching the same film over and over again and playing the same video games for hours.

All of these children have varying degrees of Autism Spectrum Disorder, which will affect their behaviour, communication skills, ability to relate to others and, in some cases, their ability to learn in the same way as typically developing children. While there is no cure for autism, there is hope for children such as those described here. With structured early intervention, consistent behaviour management, and speech and language intervention, many individuals with autism lead productive lives.

Today, many treatments for autism are available. While some of those treatments are controversial, others are based on years of sound scientific research. However, most professionals agree that each child with autism is unique and has his or her own set of strengths and weaknesses, and each child falls somewhere on a spectrum having a few more or a few less of certain characteristics than other children. This book will explain autism in simple terms, discuss the major characteristics associated with autism and offer some simple strategies for helping children with autism function in an early years setting.

The following statement sums it up best: 'Autism isn't something a person has, or a "shell" someone is trapped inside. There is no normal child hidden behind the autism…Autism is a way of being' (Jim Sinclair, 1993).

CHAPTER 1

Putting all the pieces together:
Understanding this puzzle called autism

How is autism defined?

Children with autism have been around much longer than the condition known as autism has had an official name. Leo Kanner first defined autism in 1943 when he published a paper describing 11 children with similar characteristics. The following year in Germany, Hans Asperger described a group of older children with behaviour issues. Although they had never met, both men used identical terms to describe the disorder.

Putting all the pieces together

The most accepted definition of autism comes from the International Classification of Diseases, 10th Edition and the American Diagnostic and Statistical Manual of Mental Disorders, Fourth Edition-Text Revision (DSM-IV-TR). These manuals are used by the American Psychological Association to diagnose and identify the characteristics of specific mental and emotional disorders. According to the DSM-IV-TR, to be diagnosed with autism, a person must demonstrate either delayed or atypical behaviours in the following categories:

- interaction with others (social interaction)
- communication (response to others)
- behaviour (examples include bizarre or stereotypical behaviours such as hand wringing or rocking back and forth).

Wing and Gould (1978) identified a triad of impairments:

- impairment of social relationships
- impairment of social communication
- impairment of imagination.

They defined autism as 'a complex development disability that typically appears during the first three years of life'.

With new research and information, more is understood about diagnosing and treating autism than ever before. Unfortunately, the more that experts learn about autism, the more they discover what is unknown about this disorder. Recent studies have demonstrated the significant difficulty of identifying the prevalence of autism in the UK, but a best accepted estimate is around 1 in 100 children.

Today, many children with autism attend early years and child care

All children can learn.

settings. Thus, child care providers need to know what they can do to help children with autism reach their full potential. What do you do when a three-year-old with autism falls on the floor kicking and screaming? How do you communicate with a child who looks away and flaps his hands? What do you do with a four-year-old who watches the ceiling fan as it rotates around and around? Whom do you call if you suspect a child in your class has autism?

Regardless of what definition is used, as you plan for a child with autism to come into your setting, you will need the following:

* up-to-date, accurate information about the primary characteristics of autism
* a strong support system that includes specialists such as early years specialists, special educational needs teachers, speech and language therapists and so on
* a positive relationship with the child's family so that together you can share the child's successes and challenges
* training in how to help with the child's behaviour, communication, social skills, self-help skills and stereotypical behaviours.

Why is it called Autism Spectrum Disorder?

If you were asked to think about a specific child in your setting and make a list of the things she did well, the things she was just learning to do and the things she needed to work on, it would seem like a simple task. Some children run faster than others, some are naturally more social, some children love the block area, while others seem enchanted by the role-play area.

In an early years setting, a child's specific strengths usually focus on the activities he enjoys because most typically developing children spend more time doing the things that are fun for them and less time doing things that are difficult. Children with autism are the same as other children in that they also have individual preferences and styles. However, those preferences are often expressed in different ways. For example, a child with autism may move, play with toys or relate to objects differently from her peers. While a typically developing child may take turns rolling a car back and forth with a friend, a child with autism may play only with red cars and instead of rolling the car along the floor, she will turn it over and spin one wheel repeatedly.

Provide toys the child enjoys.

Autism is described as a spectrum disorder because children with autism have characteristics that fall into a spectrum from very mild to quite severe. When discussing a child with autism, the recent literature will refer to him as having Autism Spectrum Disorder, or ASD, which means the child falls somewhere along a continuum between very severe and very mild. The child's place on the continuum helps determine how to plan for his learning. Because it is a continuum, a child may be at the mild end in terms of ability to learn new skills, and at the severe end in terms of behaviour around other children.

> Children with autism are the same as other children in that they also have individual preferences and styles. However, those preferences are often expressed in different ways.

Generally, a single child is described as having an Autism Spectrum Disorder, and a group of children are described as having Autism Spectrum Disorders. For the purposes of this book, the term *autism* refers to a child who has an Autism Spectrum Disorder.

While each child with autism is unique, it is generally agreed that all children with Autism Spectrum Disorders have difficulty in varying levels of:

- language and communication
- social relationships
- response to sensory stimuli.

In addition, these children usually will display behaviours that are not typical of their peers. For example, many young children with autism have gaps in their development ranging from learning skills out of sequence to fixation on objects such as a puzzle or a rotating fan.

Autism – the myths

Before discussing what autism is, it is important to look at some myths about autism that persist, including:

Autism is contagious. While there is research showing that autism sometimes runs in families, it is not contagious. Children cannot catch it from each other like they catch a cold.

Autism only affects boys. Even though it is four times more common in males than in females, autism affects both genders.

Autism is caused by aloof parents who are emotionally unresponsive. Bad or inattentive parenting does not cause autism.

Children with autism are always mean and hurt others. Children with autism are not always aggressive and mean. In fact, many children with autism are very timid and, if anything, are more likely to hit or hurt themselves than they are to harm others.

Children with autism never learn to communicate and play with other children. Communication is often difficult for children with autism, and many children learn alternative ways to communicate and play. However, most children with autism can learn to communicate.

Children with autism are always unhappy and cry a lot. While crying and tantrums are seen in children with autism, they can be seen as a way of the child expressing her needs/feelings.

Children with autism live in their own worlds all the time. Obsession with objects and movement or intense special interests are often seen in children with autism. However, when engaged and involved in an activity, they often interact and respond like other children.

Children with autism don't like to be touched. Tactile sensitivity is common in children with autism. However, many children enjoy a hug and being close to the people in their worlds.

All children with autism have genius-like talents, such as playing the piano or solving mathematical equations. Highly-developed talents at a young age are present in a very small number of children with autism and are not seen in most children with autism.

Each child is unique.

Children with autism die young. Left untreated, a child with autism will never reach his full potential. However, autism is not a degenerative condition; it will not get worse as the child grows older. In fact, the opposite is true. Many people with autism learn to function better as they grow older.

Words, words, words – why is there so much autism-related jargon?

It is often very confusing to read about autism, because of all the terms associated with it. With all the responsibilities that go with teaching young children, the last thing a teacher needs to be saddled with is a dictionary to learn about a child's condition. For example, a speech and language therapist tells the practitioner working with a group of three-year-olds that a young boy with autism needs to stop using *echolalia* and learn to use functional communication. After searching the Internet to decipher what she was referring to, the practitioner learns that echolalia is a term that simply means repeating everything that is heard.

This book will help to explain autism, as it relates to young children, without using jargon. When a specific term is used, it will be explained in simple terms. Definitions of key terms are provided at the end of each chapter, and most chapters include specific strategies or activities that you can use in your classroom. Most of these activities take very little time and cost almost nothing to make. It is important that as you try to understand a

child with autism, you view him as a special and unique person with talents, strengths and potential. These reminders focus on what the child can learn, rather than what can't be learned.

- **Always put the child first.** He is a child with autism, not an autistic child. Also, remember that he has a name and should be called by his name as much and as often as possible.
- **Each child is unique,** and while she may have characteristics typical of other children with autism, she will have other characteristics that are not.
- **Look for information about autism from a reliable source and remember that there may be more than one way to solve an autism-related problem.**
- **There is no single method, intervention programme that can cure or fix autism.** While many methods have been tried and are successful with some children, they may not be successful with others.

Interacting with peers

- **Learning about autism is** a process of gathering information and making informed choices based on the needs of the individual child. The National Autistic Society is the UK's leading charity for people with autism and their families. It provides information, support and services as well as campaigning for a better understanding of autism.

What are the major types of Autism Spectrum Disorder?

DSM-IV-TR classifies autism-related disorders into a single broad category referred to as Pervasive Developmental Delay (PDD). The terms Pervasive Developmental Delay and Autism Spectrum Disorder (ASD) are sometimes used interchangeably in current literature, and essentially they have the same meaning.

The recognised types of Autism Spectrum Disorder include:

- autism
- Pervasive Developmental Disorder Not Otherwise Specified (PDDNOS)
- Asperger's Syndrome
- Pathological Demand Avoidance Syndrome.

Autism

The National Autistic Society describes autism as 'a lifelong developmental disability affecting how you communicate and interact with other people'. To be diagnosed with autism, a child must exhibit significant difficulty in three areas, sometimes known as 'the triad of impairments'. They are:

- difficulty with social interaction
- difficulty with social communication
- difficulty with social imagination.

Pervasive Developmental Disorder Not Otherwise Specified (PDDNOS)

This classification is used when it is determined that a child has autism, although the characteristics displayed by the child are not like the characteristics of other children with autism. This diagnosis is also used when the onset of the disorder happens after age three. Of all the classifications used for autism, this is the most vague and confusing for families and professionals. However, this classification allows a child with a few, but not all, of the characteristics of autism to be classified as having autism so that he can receive the services he needs.

Asperger's Syndrome

Children with Asperger's Syndrome traditionally behave much like children with other types of autism when they are young, in that they will have some difficulty with communication, social interaction and/or behaviours. However, as they grow into middle school age or in adolescence, they often learn how to socialise, communicate and behave in a more socially appropriate manner. Most children with Asperger's have average or above average intelligence, so they learn new skills as fast or, in many cases, faster than their peers without autism. These children have been described as having difficulty with coordination, vocal tone (they may speak in a monotone), depression, reaction to change, and they have a tendency for

ritualistic behaviours. In addition, children with Asperger's Syndrome may develop intense obsessions with objects or activities. Unlike other children with ASD, these children tend to develop normally in the areas of self-help and adaptive behaviours, with the only exception appearing in the area of social skills, which is often delayed.

Pathological Demand Avoidance Syndrome

This condition is a recently recognised Autism Spectrum Disorder. Children with PDA avoid demands made by others because of intense feelings of anxiety when they are not in control.

Autism is very often diagnosed alongside other conditions, such as learning difficulties, dyslexia and attention deficit hyperactivity disorder (ADHD).

When and how is autism diagnosed?

Some children with autism are diagnosed by the time they are two years of age. For others, the symptoms are not recognised until they are older. Autism is, however, a medical diagnosis and requires a full examination by a qualified paediatrician. The assessment is often completed by a team of child development specialists including a psychologist and a speech and language therapist. While many paediatricians are hesitant to diagnose a child younger than two, there are benefits to an early diagnosis. The sooner a child starts receiving treatment, the better her prognosis is likely to be.

Some children will be initially assessed using a screening interview called CHAT (Checklist for Autism in Toddlers). This is not a diagnostic tool but may identify behaviours that could suggest a possible diagnosis of Autism Spectrum Disorder. A full assessment is then made by a multi-disciplinary team.

What do I need to know about children with autism?

The most important thing to know is that the sooner a child with autism receives sound, consistent and appropriate services, the better his chance of success. While there is still much to learn about how to help young children with autism and particularly how to help them adapt to a world that is

constantly changing, we know that working closely with parents and other professionals can lead to positive results.

Despite all that is known, there is still much to learn about autism and its effects on children. However, experts do agree on two things: autism cannot be cured, and there is no plan or programme that will completely eliminate all of the characteristics of the disorder. Programmes addressing the characteristics of autism while combining the medical and educational needs of the child are most effective.

Most professionals working with children with autism agree that successful interventions combine sound, structured step-by-step educational plans with developmentally appropriate practices. To help a child with autism maximise his potential, it is critical for families to play an important decision-making role in planning for the education of their child. Today, scientists from major research universities, such as Harvard, London, and Nottingham, are exploring what happens inside the brain of a child with autism. Using modern technology, such as Positron Emission Tomography (PET), researchers are, for the first time, able to look at the electrical energy within the brain to determine what part of the brain is responsible for certain actions and behaviours.

> To help a child with autism maximise his potential, it is critical for families to play an important decision-making role in planning for the education of their child.

Increasingly, these researchers are finding evidence of a disruption or change in the brains of children with autism that is not seen in their typically developing peers. Other scientists are finding that in the brain of a child with autism, serotonin is broken down and used differently. In simple terms, in the brain of a typically developing child, connections are made between brain cells. Much like a computer takes in and puts out data, these connections carry information among the parts of the brain and between other parts of the body and the brain. In children with autism, these pathways, or information connections, within the brain are made differently. This could explain why children with autism often respond to sensory input so differently from their peers.

While research hopefully will lead to new and better techniques for working with children with autism, for now, practitioners want to know what to do with a child who has autism, how to help the child control her behaviour, and what plans work best so the child can learn to communicate,

Developmentally appropriate activity

play and interact meaningfully with peers. This book is designed to help everyone working with young children to understand autism and enable them to plan for the success of all children, especially those with Autism Spectrum Disorder. Children with Autism Spectrum Disorder display a range of behaviours and abilities from very mild to quite severe. In other words, the term autism can describe a child who fits anywhere within that range. Therefore, for the purposes of this book, *autism* will be used to describe all children within that spectrum. The first step in the planning process is to examine more closely the characteristics seen in a young child with autism and learn how that child relates to the world around him.

Key terms

Autism: A complex lifelong developmental disability that typically appears during the first three years of life. Autism affects how a person communicates with, and relates to, other people and the world around them.

Autism Spectrum Disorder (ASD): Autism Spectrum Disorder (ASD) is a broad term which includes the classical form of autism as well as several related disabilities that share many of the same characteristics including difficulty with communication, socialisation and imagination. It is called spectrum because autism and autism-related characteristics range from very mild to very severe.

Developmentally appropriate practices: Activities and educational experiences that match the child's stage of development.

Echolalia: The echoing and repetition of a phrase or word.

Individual Education Plan (IEP): A personalised plan for a child designed by a team, including the child's parents, which outlines the educational goals and objectives for the child over a period of time (usually one school year).

CHAPTER 2

From hand flapping to obsession with routines:

The way children with autism relate to their worlds

What can I expect a pre-school child with autism to do?

Generally, children with autism will have varying levels of difficulty in one or more of the following areas:

- maladaptive behaviours or behaviours not typical of their peers
- stereotypic behaviours
- self-injurious behaviours
- obsessions
- rituals
- tantrums
- language and communication
- developing social relationships – especially with peers

Certain behaviours are expressions of anxiety or anger.

- responses to noise, smell, light or other sensory stimuli
- self-help or life skills, such as going to the toilet or washing their hands
- medical problems due to poor eating habits or the inability to let someone know when they are hurt or ill.

What exactly is maladaptive behaviour?

By definition, maladaptive behaviour is a behaviour that is not common in most children or a behaviour that is so severe that it interferes with learning. Some maladaptive behaviours that children with autism might have include:

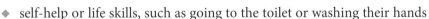

- stereotypic behaviour, such as repetitive hand flapping or saying the same phrase repeatedly
- behaviours that are self-injurious, such as hitting or biting themselves
- obsession with objects, such as collecting spoons or watching the spinning of a washing machine drum
- following rituals, such as only walking on the floor instead of carpet or having to arrange food in a certain order
- tantrums and frustration beyond those normally seen in children at this developmental stage.

What is stereotypic behaviour?

Stereotypic behaviour is usually defined as a behaviour that is carried out repeatedly and involves either movement of the child's body or movement of an object. Some of the most common stereotypic behaviours seen in young children with autism include flapping one or both hands, pulling or tapping the ears, rocking back and forth or from side to side, sniffing the air, or sucking on the upper lip. One theory about these behaviours is that children may use them to 'tune out' the world around them because they find certain noises over-stimulating. That is, the behaviour gives them internal pleasure and helps them deal with the overwhelming influences of light, sound and smell. Another, opposite theory is that the child demonstrates these behaviours because she is under-stimulated and the stereotypic behaviours increase stimulation.

Stereotypic behaviour may be a way the child calms herself. As she soothes herself by moving or rocking, her brain releases a chemical called beta-endorphin. Beta-endorphins help the body calm down and relax. Another possibility that is supported by research is that stereotypic behaviours may be a way children with autism communicate with adults and other children to control their environments. This is especially true when the child has limited or no language. When a child demonstrates these stereotypic behaviours, it may elicit attention or interaction from an adult. The adult then attends to the child or tries to stop her from doing this unusual behaviour. Over time, the child uses the stereotypic behaviour to get attention. Using stereotypic behaviour as a way of communicating with others may interfere with more appropriate development of language and communication.

Stereotypic behaviour is not usually harmful in itself. However, it often interferes with a child's ability to focus on what is going on around her. Occasionally, all children tune out activities they want to avoid. Even very young children will pretend not to hear when told it is time to stop playing. However, unlike typically developing children, children with autism learn that by doing a specific thing, such as rocking their body from side to side, they can temporarily tune out everything around them; it allows them to move further and further into their own world and further and further away from reality.

Why would a child want to injure herself?

Injuring oneself on purpose, or self-injurious behaviour, is very different from stereotypic behaviour. While a child may use stereotypic behaviour to soothe herself, or when she is happy, the same child may hit herself repeatedly when she wants to avoid a specific activity or to get something that she wants. Self-injurious behaviour is something a child does to hurt herself in an effort to get out of a situation or an environment that is overwhelming. Self-injurious behaviours include:

Using stereotypic behaviour as a way of communicating with others may interfere with more appropriate development of language and communication.

◆ biting
◆ scratching (the most common places are the hand or the top of the head)
◆ head banging
◆ squeezing parts of the body, until they bruise
◆ pinching parts of the body (usually the arm or hand).

Some experts believe these behaviours occur when a child is sick, such as when she has an ear infection. Other researchers feel that self-injury is a type of seizure over which the child has no control. Regardless of why it happens, self-injurious behaviours must be stopped immediately. Although it is rare, some self-injurious behaviours can cause permanent damage. Whenever a child starts to injure herself, it is very important that the practitioners do whatever is necessary to stop the behaviour as quickly as possible. For this reason, it is a good idea to have a plan of action already in place. Strategies must be in place to help the child become calmer. A special quiet area in the room where the child with autism can go is also helpful if the child

A quiet area is essential.

begins an activity that might cause her to injure herself. This area should have dim, indirect light, and a comfortable place to sit. The quiet area should never be used as a time-out area; it is available for the child to relax and escape the sensory overload she is experiencing.

Why do children with autism become obsessed with objects?

It is natural for a young child to be attached to an object, such as a blanket or a favourite toy. This attachment helps the child feel comfortable in new environments. Sometimes, when her favourite toy is nearby it helps her to cope with all the stress of dealing with other people. Most children outgrow the attachment as they grow more social and learn how to express their feelings and desires. Children with autism often develop attachments to objects or toys in a very different way from other children. For example, a child with autism may develop an attachment to a spoon, a rock or even the lid of a peanut butter jar. Their attachments tend to be associated with items or objects to which their peers would not become attached.

Unlike other children, who forget about their favourite toy or blanket as soon as something new and novel gets their attention, children with autism remain obsessed with their object for hours, days or even years. In addition, the object of the obsession usually serves no functional purpose. For example, Nicole enjoys her red car because she can make it go fast on the road she built with her blocks, but as soon as she gets to pre-school and sees other types of cars and trucks, she forgets about her red car and plays with the new toys. In contrast, Ellen, a child with autism, might be obsessed with a specific red car because she can make the left front wheel spin around repeatedly. Ellen will spend a long time spinning the left front wheel over and over. When Ellen gets to pre-school, she will only play with that red car (the object of her obsession) and she will only spin the left front wheel. Regardless of what other toys are introduced, Ellen will only play with one particular red car and, then, only with a specific part of the red car.

Why do children with autism follow rituals?

No one really knows why children with autism seem compelled to follow rituals. These rituals may involve an everyday activity, such as brushing teeth or washing hands. They may include things like placing all the blocks in a certain order, getting upset when books on a shelf are not arranged by size, or if a page in a special book is bent. Regardless of what the ritual is, it can become very disruptive in the early years setting.

Some rituals become compulsive, which means the child will perform them repeatedly, stopping, and beginning again, if a certain step is not performed exactly the same way every time. Some researchers feel that these rituals are the child's attempt to control a world that, to her, seems out of control. Others feel it is due to the lack of a chemical in the brain called serotonin. When a child is carrying out one of these rituals, she may seem to be indifferent to the world around her and will often get very upset if this ritual or routine is interrupted for any reason.

> Some researchers feel that these rituals are the child's attempt to control a world that, to her, seems out of control. Others feel it is due to the lack of a chemical in the brain called serotonin.

When does a typical tantrum become an autism-related tantrum?

Most early years practitioners can describe what a typical two-year-old tantrum looks like. The tantrums that children with autism have are very much like those of their typically developing peers, with one exception. Typically developing children usually start to outgrow their tantrums by the time they are in pre-school and/or they can be distracted by other activities, while children with autism may display tantrums much more intensely, for much longer and with much more energy than other children. The root cause of the tantrum may be too much environmental stimulation, such as too many sounds. These tantrums may also be triggered by things such as changes in a child's typical routine, changes in her physical environment (a parent rearranges toys in her room while cleaning), or the absence of usual or familiar people (the child's key person is replaced by another). Some researchers believe that a tantrum occurs when a child with autism goes into sensory overload.

Regardless of the cause, the tantrum is the child's attempt to convey that she is upset, unhappy, frustrated and anxious about something. Remember,

many young children with autism do not communicate their wants and needs like other children, so they may have no other way to let you know they are upset. Once a child with autism has reached the full-blown tantrum stage, there is little, if anything, that you can do but try to keep the child from hurting herself or others. For that reason, the best way to handle a child with autism who has tantrums is to prevent the tantrum by learning what events or actions cause it to occur. It is always good to remember that being proactive (preventing) is much easier than being reactive!

What is aggressive behaviour and how do I handle it?

Aggressive behaviour is behaviour that is harmful to others, such as biting, hitting, slapping, kicking, pinching or pulling hair. Many children with autism are never aggressive towards others. However, when a child is overly tired or overly stimulated her only way to protest is to strike what is nearest to her. Aggressive behaviour sometimes occurs because it is at least temporarily effective in allowing the child to get something she wants or needs (a favourite toy that another child has) or it allows the child to escape or avoid something she doesn't like (the child becomes aggressive during bath time and the bath is cut short).

Often, when a child with autism is aggressive towards others, it is because she is communicating a message that her stress level is too high. What the child is really saying in the only way she knows how is, 'HELP! STOP! NO!' (For more in-depth information on behaviour strategies, see Chapter 5.)

How do I know what a child with autism is trying to communicate with her behaviour?

It is very difficult when you do not know what a child is trying to communicate. As the child's frustration at what is going on around her increases, so does your frustration. (For more in-depth information on communication strategies, see Chapter 6.)

Often, when a child with autism is aggressive toward others, it is because she is communicating a message that her stress level is too high.

When you do not understand what the child is trying to say to you through her behaviour, ask yourself the following questions:

What was the child doing immediately before the behaviour started? For example, if Aaron was sitting down for small group time and suddenly

stands up and begins to scream, examine what happened immediately before the outburst. Perhaps you stopped interacting with Aaron and began talking to the group. If tantrums tend to occur during group activities, it may indicate that Aaron is using the tantrum to regain your attention.

What in the environment might have triggered the outburst or tantrum? Did something make a loud noise? Did it suddenly get brighter in the classroom? Is there a new smell that is unfamiliar to the child? Let's look at another example. Every time the bell rings, signalling the end of the school day, Maria screams. Once the teacher recognises this, she can give Maria headphones to wear when the bell rings.

What is the child trying to say by her behaviour? Remember, sometimes a child will act a certain way to protest, while other times she may cry out as a way of saying, 'I don't want to stop yet!' or 'There's too much going on here, I can't think!' One key to the purpose or function of a child's behaviour is to look at what may consistently (typically) happen after the child's behaviour. If the child's tantrum is often followed by some kind of interaction with the adult (even if that attention or interaction appears negative), it may be that the child is communicating (in a maladaptive way) that she wants that person's attention.

Is there something I can do to predict when the child will behave in a certain way? The behaviours of children with autism are not always predictable or logical. However, sometimes knowing what will happen next can prevent an outburst. If Candice starts biting herself every day after you come inside from the playground, it is safe to assume that she found something enjoyable outside and does not want to come inside. Based on this observation, you can cue her with a sign or special signal, right before it is time to come inside. This gives the child time to prepare

Interaction builds social skills.

herself for stopping what she enjoys and helps her prepare to come inside.

Many children with autism learn to talk, while others remain non verbal. However, just because a child does not talk, it does not mean she cannot

learn to communicate. There are several alternative or augmentative forms of communication that children with autism can use. These include:

◆ signs and symbols
◆ communication pictures: these are pictures that the child points to when she wants to say what is happening or what she needs or wants
◆ communication devices: computer-like devices that speak for the child and are activated when he pushes a button or selects a picture.

For more information about communication and descriptions of how children with autism communicate and strategies for helping children communicate more effectively, see Chapter 6.

What do I do when a child won't interact with others?

Whether it is making eye contact or looking at someone when they speak, it is safe to say that most children with autism do not interact with other people the same as their typically developing peers. The ability to interact varies with each child, and some children with Asperger's Syndrome learn to fake it at a very young age. In other words, they learn that if they pretend to attend to a person, or minimally interact by saying, 'Hi', or waving goodbye, then people will leave them alone. However, for the most part, children with autism do not start or initiate interactions and often will do almost anything to avoid having to interact with someone. For this reason, social skills training and learning how to respond in social situations should begin as early as possible and should be an ongoing goal throughout the child's education.

It is important to remember to work with the child's parents and other carers to prioritise the order in which social skills are taught, as trying to teach the child too many new skills without enough time for practice can be overwhelming. The result may be that the child becomes more withdrawn and is more likely to exhibit a maladaptive behaviour in social situations. There are strategies that can be used to encourage social interaction that are discussed in detail in Chapter 8.

> Social skills training and learning how to respond in social situations should begin as early as possible and should be an ongoing goal throughout the child's education.

Why do children with autism have difficulty with sensory stimuli?

Children learn very early how to respond to their environment by using
their senses. When only a few months old, a baby
learns to recognise her mother by her smell or the
sound of her voice. We have all seen a child smack
her lips when she smells a favourite food. When
something is too loud, a toddler puts her hands
over her ears as a signal to 'turn down the noise'.
Unfortunately, unlike other children, children with
autism are not able to filter out and respond to
information that they receive through their senses.
To a child with autism, a fluorescent overhead light,
commonly found in many early years settings, can
often have the same effect that a powerful flashing
strobe light might have on a typically developing

Holding a favourite toy helps a child stay focused.

child. In addition, the soft ticking of a clock or the hum of a computer might
sound entirely different to a child with autism.

Children typically love to touch new objects. The common feely box
that many practitioners use to introduce new textures can be torture to
a child with autism. In other words, for a typically developing child, her
body is much like a computer in that it is a sensory processing machine. By
the time a child is two or three, she learns how to filter sound and how to
ignore unimportant sounds in the background. For children with autism,
the information they receive from their environment can become distorted
and may not be reliable. For this reason, most children with autism have
some form of sensory integration disorder. That means they cannot filter
or screen out sensory related things. Sensory integration is discussed further
in Chapter 9.

Can children with autism learn basic problem-solving skills?

Children with autism are similar to their peers in that they have varying
degrees of problem-solving skills. While many children with autism have
learning difficulties, do not assume that all children with autism are
cognitively impaired or delayed. While some children with autism perform

Children learn best when they are relaxed.

much like children with developmental delays, many do not. In fact, there are children with autism who are quite skilled at solving complex problems, and will go to great lengths to work out a solution to a difficult problem.

When trying to teach a new skill or a problem-solving task, it is best to keep in mind the following:

- Just like other children, a child with autism learns best when she is rested and relaxed.
- Because change is so difficult, tell the child when you begin to teach her something new. If possible, show her a picture of what she will be doing.
- Introduce a new skill in small steps and provide the child multiple opportunities to practise.
- Most children with autism have difficulty with generalisation. That means that while they may be able to perform a skill in one setting or with one person, they may not be able to do the same task in another environment or with someone who is unfamiliar to them.
- Most importantly, children with autism can and do learn new tasks and skills. However, they may learn them in a way that is unique.

Why do children with autism only eat certain foods?

Sometimes, children with autism will only eat certain foods. For example, they may only eat pizza with cheese or only eat orange jelly. Often, this obsession with certain foods lasts a lifetime, while sometimes it is temporary. These obsessions can be preferential, meaning that, while they prefer one food over other foods, the child will eat non-preferred foods. Other children are more absolute in their diet, meaning they will only eat certain foods to the exclusion of all others. This type of eating behaviour creates challenges at home and at school.

How do I know if a child with autism is unwell?

While we as practitioners are not supposed to diagnose or treat the physical illnesses of the children in our care, we should alert parents when we suspect that a child is unwell or hurt. Autism-related behaviours could

mask when a child is ill. For example, Rebecca, a three-year-old in the class, is usually very social and outgoing. Today, instead of going to the creative activity (her personal favourite), she goes to the back of the room, lies on the floor and closes her eyes, or, during small group time, Rebecca puts her hands over her ears and lays her head on the table.

What would you do? The answer is easy. Rebecca's key person would recognise that something is wrong and that Rebecca is not feeling well. In fact, you might ask, 'Rebecca, do your ears hurt?' or 'Do you feel okay?' When Rebecca's mother comes to pick her up, you would tell her that you suspect Rebecca may be unwell. However, for a child with autism, you have no way to know how she is feeling, what is hurting, and more importantly, whether something is hurting that day that did not hurt the day before.

While it is challenging and difficult, try to remember that children with autism get ill and need medical attention as much as their typically developing peers; they often do not receive it because their autism interferes with the child getting an accurate diagnosis. For example, Zoe hits herself and is prone to intense tantrums. Every time her mother takes her to the doctor, she has a tantrum and begins to hit herself repeatedly. Because of these behaviours, it may be very difficult for the doctor to diagnose a stomach problem. Zoe not only cannot tell the doctor where she hurts (pains in the stomach), the doctor also cannot get close enough to examine her stomach, because Zoe is hitting and screaming. If it were less difficult for the doctor to examine her, it would be easier to see that Zoe has issues with trapped wind. Medication might ease her pains, thus reducing her tantrums and hitting. Being more aware of the possibility that the child may be in pain or physically ill is the first step to being more responsive to the child and less responsive to the autism itself.

Being more aware of the possibility that the child may be in pain or physically ill is the first step to being more responsive to the child and less responsive to the autism itself.

How do I assess a child with autism?

While a multi-disciplinary team are responsible for assessing a child for the purpose of diagnosis, early years practitioners typically assess for other reasons. For example, a practitioner may assess a child with

Top: Sample portfolio
Bottom: Sample anecdotal record

autism to determine her progress in a setting or to help decide how to plan goals and objectives appropriate for her age and stage of development. As might be expected, children with autism may not score well on standard early childhood checklists. Detailed observation is the key to accurate assessment and the foundation of effective planning.

Because the objective of an assessment is to demonstrate a child's progress over time, the best form of assessment for a child with autism is a portfolio. Portfolios are collections of the child's work over a specific period and are not intended to be giant scrapbooks representing all the child's work. Instead, a portfolio should highlight a child's best efforts across specific areas. Since children with autism tend to develop at a pace that is quite different from their peers, the portfolio is a way of demonstrating and documenting that change. An additional benefit of the portfolio is that it allows the practitioner to see and document skills as they emerge. By knowing when a skill is emerging, the practitioner can plan learning that will encourage the child to continue developing that specific skill.

With access to a digital camera it is possible to load samples of a child's work onto a CD for documentation in an electronic portfolio. This can be shared with the child's parents. The electronic portfolio can be used to share information between settings. This eliminates the need to store a quantity of materials, and provides a convenient way for the child's family to see evidence of progress.

Another method of assessment used for young children with autism is the anecdotal record. These are ongoing notes made by the practitioner about a child's behaviour or performance of a task. Anecdotal records are especially effective in documenting the events leading up to, or following, a particular behaviour. An efficient way to keep an anecdotal record is to punch holes in the upper right hand corner of several index cards and keep

them on a ring. This way, the practitioner can hang the ring on a hook for easy retrieval and use. Notes written immediately following an event are usually more accurate than notes based on memory. In addition, anecdotal notes can serve as documentation to help plan new activities for the child.

The learning characteristics of children with autism summarised

Now that you know how a child with autism relates to her world, it is time to set up an environment that is proactive. A proactive environment is ready for the child with autism and is prepared to help that child make the most of her early years experiences. The table below is a summary of characteristics associated with autism.

Tuning out the world

Summary of the basic characteristics associated with autism

Characteristic	How the child might act
Undesired behaviours (maladaptive)	◆ Constant or repetitive behaviour such as waving hands or hand flapping ◆ Hitting self or others ◆ Tantrums ◆ Aggressive towards others
Lack of functional communication	◆ Echolalia ◆ Stereotypic phrases ◆ Nonsense speech ◆ No speech/language
Problems with social interaction	◆ Only interacts when something is needed ◆ Interacts with objects, not people ◆ Preoccupation with things, not people ◆ Totally in her own world
Obsessions	◆ Rituals ◆ Routines that must be followed ◆ Only eats specific types of foods ◆ May be obsessed with objects such as spoons

Key terms

Anecdotal record: Ongoing notes made by the teacher concerning a child's behaviour or performance of a task.

Augmentative forms of communication: An alternative way to communicate, such as a device that speaks for the child.

Beta-endorphin: A chemical in the brain that helps the body relax.

Compulsive: Behaviours the child performs repeatedly that will be stopped and begun again, if a certain step is not performed exactly the same way every time.

Cue: A hint that is a word, gesture or phrase.

Generalisation: Being able to perform the same task, skill or activity in a variety of settings or with a variety of people and/or different objects.

Life skills: Self-help skills, such as going to the toilet or washing hands.

Maladaptive behaviour: A behaviour that is not common in most children or one that is so severe that it interferes with learning.

Obsession: A strong inclination towards something to the point of excluding everything else, such as collecting spoons or watching the blades of a rotating ceiling fan.

Portfolio: A collection of the child's best work across a specific period. The portfolio is not intended to represent all the child's work; it should showcase a child's best efforts across specific areas.

Ritual: A pattern or way of doing something that is not logical, such as only walking on the floor instead of carpet or having to arrange food in a certain order before it can be eaten.

Self-injurious behaviour: Something a child does to hurt herself, such as hitting or biting herself, in an effort to get out of a situation or an environment that is overwhelming.

Sensory integration disorder: An inability to filter or screen out sensory-related input.

Stereotypic behaviour: A behaviour that is carried out repeatedly and involves either movement of the child's body or movement of an object, such as repetitive hand flapping or saying the same phrase repeatedly.

Tantrum: Anger beyond what is normally seen in children, such as falling to the floor and screaming or throwing their bodies on the ground.

CHAPTER 3

Planning for success:

Setting up a proactive pre-school environment

I know children with autism learn differently, but what can I do about it?

The best way to prepare to help a child with autism is to get to know as much as possible about the child before he comes into the setting. Encourage the child and his family to visit before the first day of school. Visit the child at home as well. These initial visits will give you time to get to know the child and give the child time to become familiar with the early years setting.

Most early years providers already have a parent information form. However, you will need to find out much more about the child than is generally included on the form.

Below are some questions you should ask before the child arrives:

Plan activities around the child's strengths.

- What does she like to eat? Are there certain foods that she will not eat or that will cause her to react in a certain way?
- What particular interests does she have?
- Does she have a particular attachment to a certain object, toy or activity?
- How does she communicate with others?
- What might cause her to become upset or frustrated?
- What do the parents think are her strengths?
- What do the parents think are her challenges?
- Who is her doctor or health visitor?
- What other services has she been getting, such as speech and language therapy?

- Are there any other children at home?
- What does the family do when she has an outburst at home?
- How much experience has she had of other children?

Some children may arrive with an Individual Education Plan (IEP) already in place. However, those plans are designed to look at broad educational objectives and goals for the child and may have been written long before he arrives in your setting. The IEP is a good tool to help you plan the child's learning. However, you also need to know as much as possible about the child and his preferences and experiences with others so that when he arrives you are prepared. If he was previously in another setting, schedule a visit to observe and gather information. Plan transition from his previous setting carefully – your goal as the child's key person is to make his transition from the previous setting to your setting as stress-free as possible for the child, the parents and yourself.

How do I arrange an early years environment for success?

The environment should be as well-defined as possible. Each activity or learning area should be clearly marked with a picture. It is also very important that you include a picture schedule or visual timetable in each area so the child can look at the schedule and get an idea of what is supposed to

A quiet area should be a place where the child can go without distraction and relax.

occur within that area. This will reduce anxiety. Remember, children with autism like to know what they are supposed to do, so a picture schedule is reassuring and helps the child adjust to her new environment.

Children with autism also need a special place in the room where they can go. This should be located in the quietest part of the room, without distractions, and without all the sensory input they receive elsewhere. The quiet place should have indirect soft lighting, a chair or cushion that is comfortable for the child and a few activities that the child likes. Make sure that you can always

observe the child in whatever location you choose. This quiet area is also a place where the child can go to complete activities that are especially stressful for him. While a quiet area is especially essential for children with autism, it should be open to all children who need time to reflect and relax before returning to an activity.

Quiet areas should never be used as a form of punishment for a child, but should be used routinely to allow the child to be in a place where he feels safe and secure. The frequency and time that a child uses the quiet area will be different, depending on the needs of the individual child.

> Remember that children with autism function best when they have:
>
> ◆ structure
> ◆ a predictable routine
> ◆ environments that are not distracting
> ◆ verbal reminders of what will happen next
> ◆ picture schedules.

How do I set up predictable routines for a child with autism that will not be boring for other children?

When setting up a daily routine for a child with autism, it is important to ensure that the child understands what you are asking him to do. Children with autism are less frustrated with predictable and organised routines. How the day begins will often determine how the child will behave throughout the day. If there is any variation in the schedule, even a minor change, it is important that the child knows before it happens.

When the child arrives, greet her and discuss the daily schedule. Interchangeable picture or photo cards can be used to show each activity for the day. Make sure the child knows what each picture card represents. Children will need a schedule on a level that they understand. For some children, this may be an object schedule, or a simple 'first–then' card. A 'first–then' card is a series of picture pairs in which the

Using a picture schedule to find out what happens next

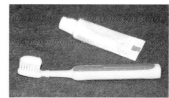

Sample 'first–then' cards

first picture shows what happens first and the second shows what happens next. Remember that picture schedules can be very simple or quite complex.

Transitions are likely times for a child with autism to find difficult. So, plan smooth transitions. Music makes an excellent transition tool. Use the same song for each transition so that the child learns that the song is a cue for something new to happen.

Other ideas to help facilitate smooth transitions include:

- Set a timer a few minutes before it's time to change activities; sand timers are less distracting than timers with bells.
- Touch the child gently on the shoulder as a cue that it is almost time to stop.
- Walk over to the picture schedule and point to the next activity.
- Ring a small chime, such as wind chimes (remember not to overwhelm with loud noises), as a reminder that it is time to change activities.
- Avoid flashing lights on and off – this is not a good method to use for signalling transition. The sensory stimulation for a child with autism will be overwhelming.

What can I do to make all children feel part of the group?

In everything you do, adopt a philosophy that values each child as a member of the group. Adopting this philosophy goes beyond using the right words or putting up pictures showing children with special needs. It means that your actions and activities demonstrate your belief that all children can learn. Build a truly inclusive support environment for the benefit of all.

When planning for children with special needs, keep these points in mind:

- **Every child is a valued member of the group.** A member of the group has the same rights and responsibilities as his classmates and the expectations for him are matched to his abilities.
- **Treat others the way you want them to treat you.** Model how to be a friend and how friends act towards each other.
- **Consistency and structure work best for children with autism.** While

flexibility is important, it is also important to remember that children with autism become very upset and frustrated when people are inconsistent with them and when schedules are disrupted.

Working together helps everyone feel part of the group.

- **Everyone can participate in some way.** Even children with severe autism and a high level of need can participate in activities.
- **All children have strengths and weaknesses.** Learn to identify a child's strengths and plan activities that are geared to enhance the areas where she is strong.
- **Nothing is free and no one is automatically entitled to anything.** Communication is perhaps the most important social skill of all. Teach children how to ask for what they want and need verbally, by using signs, with gestures or pointing, or a picture exchange communication system.
- **Learned helplessness cannot be tolerated.** In other words, just because a child has special needs or is challenged in some way does not mean that he cannot learn to be as independent as possible. When everything is done for a child he will learn how to be helpless and automatically expect the adults in his world to do things for him.

Water play is a fun group activity.

- **Children learn from each other.** Arrange the environment so that children have many opportunities to practise new skills, work in groups, and depend on each other to help solve problems.
- **Bullying, and making fun of others are never acceptable.** What may seem like simple childish teasing can soon become bullying, which can be frightening for any child, and especially children with autism, who are very literal.
- **Many times, misbehaviours are just misdirected attempts to communicate.** When a child throws an object or has a tantrum, look at the reason behind the action. Although the behaviour is not acceptable, the reason for the behaviour may be explainable and is often avoidable.

Getting started

This strategy works best if you can use it before the first day that the new child is in your setting.

What to do

1. When you learn that a child with autism will be starting in your setting, contact the parents and ask them to share as much information as possible to help your planning.

2. Arrange to meet the parents. When they arrive, be positive and tell them you are excited about having their child (use his name) in your group. Assure them that the meeting is about planning together for his success in pre-school.

3. When meeting with the parents, encourage them to bring along others who work with the child as well, such as grandparents, babysitters or extended family members. Start the meeting on a positive note and tell them you are counting on them to help you. Assure them that you hope pre-school will be a positive experience for them and their child.

4. Ask them about their child. Listen. Remember that the child will be with you for only a few hours each day, but he is with his family the majority of the time. Parents know their children best. Even if the parents have unrealistic expectations for their child, it is not up to you to make predictions as to what can and what cannot be accomplished.

5. Avoid making promises you cannot keep, such as, 'I promise Tom will have a great year and make many new friends.' Instead, say, 'I hope Tom will have a great year. I will try to help him make friends.'

6. Educate yourself about the child's diagnosis. Find out as much as you can about the child's routine and how he learns best. Avoid falling into

the trap of trying to cure the child. Instead, look for ways to help him develop his strengths.

7. Begin the year with a commitment to yourself always to tell the parents one positive thing that their child has done before you discuss any issues.

8. Remember to take notes throughout the meeting. Jot down any questions you might want to ask before the parents leave.

9. Set an example for others in your setting or school by always using people-first language and referring to the child as a child 'with autism'. For example, avoid describing or referring to the child as, 'the autistic child'. Don't refer to the child's problems – instead, talk about the weaknesses as challenges.

Helpful hints

♦ Don't be too hard on yourself. You will make mistakes, but you will also learn a lot in the process.

♦ Remember that working with children is stressful, and that working with children with special needs can add to that stress. Take care of yourself. Learn to take a deep breath, relax and keep the challenges in perspective.

♦ Ask for help. Asking someone to help you with a child's behaviour or with differentiating the curriculum shows that you are experienced enough to know when you need extra support.

♦ If you focus on the child's abilities, rather than his disabilities, your experience will be much more enjoyable.

Laying the foundations: starting from day one

Try to anticipate the needs and preferences of the child before he arrives, bearing in mind that there will always be things you did not anticipate.

What to do

1. Study your notes from the initial parent meeting and any other information you have received about the child.
2. Make a list of the child's preferences. Include his favourite story, songs and activities. Remove or eliminate things that may make him uncomfortable, like certain noises or smells. If you find out the name of his pet(s) or sibling(s), write it/them down for future reference.
3. Go through each area of your setting and do an environmental check.
4. Ask yourself the following questions: Are there activities she might enjoy? Have I designated a quiet place for her to get away and calm down, if needed? Is each area clearly marked with a picture so that it is easily identifiable? Have I made a picture schedule of what will happen throughout the day and is it posted in a prominent place?
5. Involve the whole early years team and particularly the key person, in every stage of planning and preparation.
6. Consider the other children in the setting. Who might be a good peer buddy for the child with autism? Who might be fearful of the child and need some guidance about how to treat peers with special needs? Will

this be the first child in your class with special needs? If so, do you need to talk to the class about valuing diversity?

7. Do you have a plan of action if any member of staff working with the child feels they need help or support?

8. Make a list of the child's medical issues, and any other concerns that will help the other adults (assistant teachers, volunteers, etc.) in your setting feel more comfortable.

9. Create and share an 'All about me' book (see page 42).

Helpful hints

◆ Try to anticipate the needs and preferences of the child before he arrives, keeping in mind that there will always be things you did not anticipate.

◆ Remember, all parents want what is best for their child, and some parents of typically developing children in the group may have fears and concerns. Answer them honestly, assuring them that all the children in your setting are valued.

◆ This may be the first time the child with autism has been in a setting with other children, and her parents may be anxious. Assure them that you will contact them, if needed.

Good morning! Good morning!

To greet the child with autism and start the day on a positive note.

What to do

1. Start each day with the same routine. It is important that you use the same words and phrases each day.
   You might try something like,
   'Good morning, (child's name).'
   Wait to see if the child responds.
   'Let's check and see what we are going to do first.'

2. Either kneel down at eye level and show the child a picture schedule of what you want him to do, or, if you are wearing a communication apron (see page 100) point out to the child what happens first.

3. If the child does not respond to a spoken welcome, he may respond to a song. Try the following, sung to the tune of 'Three Blind Mice' (first verse).

   (child's name) *welcome,*
   (child's name) *welcome,*
   I'm glad you're here.
   I'm glad you're here.

4. Direct the child to his peg. If he hesitates, walk with him and show him. Put a picture of the child above his peg to help him identify it more easily.

5. Tell him what to do next: 'After you hang your coat on your peg, go to the _____ activity.'

6. Say or sign, 'Thank you.'

7. If the child does not move independently to an activity, walk with him. Show him the picture cards that relate to hanging up his coat, and so on, and then guide him to the activity where he will begin his day.

8. A child with autism likes structure and set routines. Even if you start the morning with a free choice of activities, direct the child to a specific starting place each morning.

9. After he is accustomed to the routine, you can vary the welcome by giving two or more activity choices.

Helpful hints

♦ Keep focused on your primary objective, which is to start each day with a calm and predictable sequence.

♦ Regardless of how you start the day, consistency will make the child with autism feel more secure.

♦ Face it, some children are just not morning people and need a little more time to wake up. If the child is prone to unsettled mornings, then begin each day by allowing him to go to his quiet place for a few minutes, until he has adjusted to the routine.

♦ Don't forget that when you are absent, it is crucial that any substitute practitioner follows the same morning welcome routine as you.

'All about me!' Notice board and book

This strategy helps the child with autism feel special and valued.

NOTICE BOARD

What to do

1. Ask parents to send some pictures of the children and their families to school. Action pictures work best, because they show the children doing things. Ask the parents to write a few sentences to go along with each picture that describe what the family is doing, and include names of the people in the pictures.

2. Feature a different child each week on the bulletin board. Put up pictures of his family and pictures of what the child enjoys.

3. After you have displayed the pictures, build an activity around them (see below). Talk about the child's siblings, pets or activities. This helps the child feel more comfortable and helps all children in the class see the child with autism as being more like them.

BOOK

What to do

1. Make an 'All about me!' book for each child in the class. Be sure to include pictures of grandparents, pets, activities and customs that the family enjoys. The child can use the book throughout the year. To make the book, collect photos of the child and the special people, pets and places in his life. Mount the photos on paper of the child's preferred colour to enhance his use and enjoyment of the book. Invite the child

to help you write a short caption or description about each photo. If the child is non verbal or has limited communication skills, ask family members to help write the captions at home. Make sure that no more than two pictures are displayed on each page because too many pictures can be overwhelming. Place each page in a plastic pocket or laminate.

Insert the sheets into a small notebook or ring binder. Ask the child to draw a picture for the cover or place a photo of the child's family on the cover. This will help the child identify his notebook.

2. Making a book about a child also helps connect his family to the setting, and it can be used to help children discover things they have in common with their peers, such as the number of brothers and sisters, types of pets, family customs, family activities and so on.

3. An additional benefit of this activity is that, as you get to know more about the child with autism and his family, you can plan activities centred on familiar things.

Helpful hints

◆ Be aware that not all children come from traditional families. Family is defined by the child and those he lives with, not by any traditional rule.

◆ Some children may be in care or come from families that are in the process of change. In this case, the 'All about me' activities might focus on what the child likes to do and what activities he enjoys at home and in the setting.

◆ It is also not uncommon for a child to be in a step family or be in a situation where he spends some time with parents in two separate households. In this case, try to include family members from both households.

Books that teach a lesson

Avoid doing this activity in groups that are so large that the child with autism is overwhelmed by the other children.

What to do

1. Books can be important tools for helping more developmentally advanced children explore themes and values.
2. Once you have identified what you want to help the child learn, such as 'try, try again', conquering fears or dealing with autism, then select a book that has that theme.
3. Whenever you read aloud, be sure to show the child that books have a title page, a beginning and an end. Let the child hold the book while you read it to her.
4. To reinforce the concept in the book, plan activities to support the book's lesson or value, and send a family letter home telling families that this week the children are learning to _____ and the book they are reading is _____.
5. Below are some books that teach common themes to which all children can relate.

Helpful hints

- If the child can't be there while you read the whole book, read only part of it. When you return to read the remainder, remember to review what has happened so far in the story.
- Before reading a book about the child's special needs, make sure his parents are in agreement.

Book	Theme	Book	Theme
Amazing Grace	Believe in yourself	*Owl Babies*	Fear
A Chair for My Mother	Cooperation, love and respect	*When My Autism Gets Too Big*	Helping children with autism
Alexander and the Terrible, Horrible, No Good, Very Bad Day	Everyone has a bad day	*The Three Little Pigs*	Working together
		Badger's Parting Gifts	Death
		Rainbow Fish	Learning to share

This list is adapted, with permission, from *Smart Start* by Pam Schiller. Additional titles added by C. Willis.

Making new friends

Let the family know that their child is working on introducing himself, so that they can help him practise at home.

What to do

1. Make a prompt card with two cues. Have one for the child's name and one to remind him to wait for the other person to respond. Laminate the cards, if possible.

My name is Jordan.

2. Explain to the child that the cards will help him know what to do when he meets someone new.

3. Ask several children to help you and the child practise meeting people.

4. Sit in a circle and practise what to say and how to wait for the person to respond.

5. Remind the children that, when you are meeting someone for the first time, it's a good idea to look at them.

6. Look for opportunities to encourage the child to practise using the prompt cards to introduce himself.

Helpful hints

◆ Later, when the child is familiar with this routine, add other cues, such as communicating something that he likes to do or asking a new friend to play a game.

◆ Remember to make a set of prompt cards for the child to take home.

◆ Let the family know that the child is working on introducing himself, so that they can help him practise.

Classroom hunt: I spy!

To encourage the child with autism to explore, to interact with new toys and to try new activities.

What to do

1. Gather items that represent each of the areas in your setting. For example, blocks from the block area, a magnetic letter from the literacy area, a paintbrush from the art area, a book from the reading corner and so on.

2. Place the items in a basket or box. A basket works well because you can carry it on your arm. The child may even be willing to carry it for you.

3. Tell the child that you need help putting the things in your basket back in the areas where they belong.

4. Start each hunt with the same phrase, 'Here is a _____. I wonder where this goes?'

5. If the child looks away or appears uninterested, try to refocus him on the item by holding it in front of him.

6. Ask, '(child's name), where do you think this goes?' (Hold up object.)

7. If he does not reply or take the object, then try to prompt him by walking to an area and saying, 'Do you think it goes here?'

8. When you and the child agree where the object belongs, ask the child to place the item in/on the correct box or shelf. Continue with the other objects in the basket.

Helpful hints

- If the child is willing, you might try to do the activity with another child as well, so that the three of you look for the correct locations.
- Vary the activity. If you are using picture cards, match the item to the picture card, before returning it to its proper location.
- Always say the name of the object.
- If the child acts uninterested or bored, try putting the object in the wrong place and see if he will correct you. Sometimes, even non verbal children have an extraordinary sense of place and know in fine detail where items are usually located.

We're more alike than different

To help other children become more tolerant of those who are different, especially children with disabilities.

What to do

1. Before beginning the activity, make a talking stick. Make one by decorating a paper towel roll, covering one end with heavy tape, adding uncooked rice or dried beans, and then covering the other end with tape. If possible, encourage each child to add something (a scrap of paper, a bit of yarn, a bit of cloth) to the talking stick until it is completely covered.
2. Place children in a small group (five or less works best). Tell them, 'Today, you are going to play a game called "This is what I like!"'
3. This game is loosely based on a Native American custom of using a talking stick, where only the person with the stick can talk.
4. Start the activity by saying, 'I am first.' Hold up the talking stick and say, 'What I like about me is _____.' Fill in the blank with something you like about yourself, such as, 'What I like about me is that I enjoy singing.' Pause, turn to the child on your right, and say, 'What I like about you is _____' (fill in the blank with something you have observed about the child). For example, 'What I like about you is that you are always kind to your friends at school.'
5. Continue to pass the stick around the circle, with all of the children saying something they like about themselves, and then something they like about the person sitting next to them.
6. If the child with autism does not participate, that is okay. However, encourage the child next to him to say something she likes about him.

Helpful hints

◆ The first time you complete this activity, place the child with autism on your right so that you can be the one to say something about him.
◆ Vary the game by adding other things such as, 'I am good at _____' or 'You are good at _____.'
◆ Encourage parents to play the game at home with their child.

Things we do together (a small group activity)

To help the child identify the various activities he will experience throughout the day.

What to do

1. Before beginning the activity, tell the children that they are going to help you play a game. You will describe something that happens in a particular area and they will tell you which activity it is.
2. Place children in small groups (five or fewer works best). Begin the activity by telling them that you are going to describe a place in the room and you want them to tell you where it is. For non verbal children, ask them to point to which area you are describing.
3. Describe an area, such as, 'I am thinking about a place where we paint pictures.'
4. Wait, and see if anyone raises a hand to answer the question. The child with autism may watch as other children answer. When it is his turn, use his name. For example, say, 'James, can you tell me or show me where we play with blocks?'
5. Continue to ask questions, until everyone has had a turn.
6. Later, when everyone is familiar with the classroom, expand the game to include questions about other places in your setting, such as, 'I am thinking about a place where we play outside' or 'I am thinking about where we go when we need to go to the toilet.'

Helpful hints

◆ The first time you play this game, place the child with autism close to you, so you can help redirect him, if necessary.

Key terms

Attend: To pay attention to or to concentrate.

Learned helplessness: When a child learns how to be helpless because he never has the opportunity to do anything for himself; instead, everything is done for him.

People-first language: Referring to the person, and then the special needs.

Picture apron: An apron worn by the teacher with pictures depicting the day's schedule.

Picture schedule or visual timetable: A series of pictures showing what is supposed to occur within an area or time-frame.

Talking stick: A sealed, decorated tube with items inside that make interesting sounds.

Transition: Moving from one activity or area to another.

CHAPTER 4

Learning self-help skills:
What are self-help skills?

Tying shoes is an important skill.

What are self-help skills?

Self-help skills have been given many names – life skills, everyday skills, independent living skills, and functional skills. Regardless of which term you use, these activities are the skills that children will use throughout their lives. They are skills that will help them function in daily activities and help them take care of themselves. Examples include going to the toilet, feeding themselves, dressing themselves, brushing their teeth, taking a bath, and learning to recognise common things around them such as toilets, exits and stop signs. As the child gets older, these skills might include learning to access community resources, such as the bank, the post office and local shops. For pre-school children, these skills usually mean those activities that help them to become more independent.

Why are self-help skills important?

Self-help skills are important for a variety of reasons. First, they help a child gain independence, making him feel more in control of his world. Predictability and routines are very important to children with autism, and the more they are able to take care of their own personal needs, the more predictable their daily life will be. Additionally, learning to take care of basic needs such as going to the toilet, washing and dressing helps the child socially. Let's face it, other children are more likely to want to interact and play with a child with good personal hygiene. Most importantly,

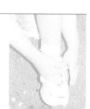

self-help skills help the child's self-esteem, by giving her a sense of accomplishment and the confidence that comes from doing it 'all by herself'.

How do I teach everyday tasks?

Work with the child's family to help determine which skills to teach first. If the skill is a high-priority skill for the child's family, they are more likely to work with him at home to learn it. When teaching any skill, it is important that you and the child's family use the same method to teach him and practise the same skill in exactly the same way. Using the same words, phrases and picture cues reinforces the new skill, making it easier to learn.

Mastering a new skill

It is important that self-help skills are taught and practised in the context of daily routines and in the environment in which that skill would be likely to arise. For example, you would not want to teach a child to brush his teeth while sitting at a table in an early years setting. Instead, you would take him to the natural environment, in this case the bathroom, where brushing his teeth would normally happen. Likewise, you would not try to teach him the steps to feeding himself at circle time. Remember that children with autism are very literal, and practising a skill in a time or place in which that skill would not normally occur is confusing for the child, and it slows down his progress in developing that skill. Because the child is so busy trying to figure out why something is being practised in a simulated or pretend way, he often fails to concentrate on what you are asking him to do. This chapter focuses on just those skills that will help the child with autism in his day-to-day routines at school.

Drying hands without help

Feeding yourself is a self-help skill.

Early years self-help skills can be grouped into these categories:

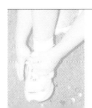

- eating and drinking
  - using utensils to eat
  - drinking from a cup or through a straw
  - simple table manners
  - social context of mealtimes
- toileting
  - asking to go to the toilet
  - taking care of own toilet needs
  - washing hands after toileting
- handling unplanned situations
- self-care
  - brushing teeth
  - washing and drying face
  - tolerating a bath
  - brushing hair
- dressing
  - getting dressed and tolerating new or different clothes
  - getting dressed to go outside
  - taking off and putting on clothes
  - learning to select clothes appropriate for the weather
- simple routines
  - getting up in the morning
  - arriving at pre-school
  - learning the daily routine
  - getting ready to go to lunch
  - getting ready to go home
- adjusting back, after a period of being out of the setting for holidays, illness and so on.

What do I do first, before teaching a new skill?

Deciding which skill to teach first involves getting input from a variety of sources and on the developmental level of the child. Begin by looking at some general guidelines to use when planning to teach any new skill.

◆ **Start by deciding which skill is the most important to the child and his family.** This decision should be based on the developmental level of the child and on the wishes of his family. It should also be based on your careful observation of the child. Trying to teach a self-help skill before the child is ready can be confusing, frustrating and frightening for the child, and could result in a delay in his learning the skill.

Pouring is a more advanced feeding skill.

◆ **Identify the challenges in teaching the skill you have selected,** such as the child's hyper-sensitivity to touch, her short attention span or the child's unwillingness to tolerate water.

◆ **Inform everyone who will be working with the child** so they are aware that plans are being made to teach something new. Don't forget to include everyone in the setting and other people with whom the child spends a significant amount of time.

◆ **Gather all the materials** you will need to teach the new skill.

◆ **Make a list of the vocabulary associated with the new skill.** Be sure to check with the child's family so that you are both using the same words and the same procedure for practising the new skill. Children with autism do best with concrete terms; make sure you are using terms that are not confusing.

◆ **Make a task analysis or step-by-step guide for completing the skill.** Write down each step and then go over the list to see if you have left off anything important. On your list, be very detailed and describe for yourself what you want the child to do.

Trying to teach a self-help skill before the child is ready can be confusing, frustrating and frightening for the child, and could result in a delay in his learning the skill.

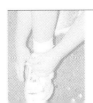

- Make another task analysis that you will use with the child. This list is much less detailed and simpler than the list you made for yourself. Be very specific, concise and clear about what the child is to do.
- Practise the skill several times yourself, using the list you have made for the child. Watch yourself as you model each step. Remember, things that seem natural to you, such as hanging up a towel after you use it or flushing a toilet, may not be natural for the child.
- Decide on the best time to begin implementation of the new skill. Even if the child is not ready to do the complete task alone, she still may be ready to start learning some of the basic steps.
- Make sequence cards for each step and use simple pictures that clearly demonstrate what you are doing. Make a second set of cards to send home. It is always good to make a third set of cards as a back-up, in case something happens to the sequence cards.
- Practise any new skill in the natural environment in which it would occur. For example, the child should practise teeth brushing at a real sink in the bathroom – not at a pretend sink. The child should learn feeding skills when she is eating, and so on. Place the sequence cards in front of the child and talk about each one. Remember to use clear, concrete language.
- Model each step for the child before asking him to start the task.
- Don't forget the home–school connection. Keep the family involved so that what is learned at school can be reinforced at home. Generalisation is often very difficult. Don't be discouraged if a skill that the child has learned at school does not immediately transfer to another environment.
- Give the child time to practise one step of a skill before going on to the next. Expecting too much, too soon, can be overwhelming for both you and the child.
- Use small steps that you are certain are achievable.

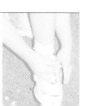

How does this all fit together?

Now that you have an idea about learning self-help skills, look at this example of a specific skill, such as brushing teeth. Terrance is a four-year-old in Lydia's room. He is not upset by water, and, in fact, Lydia has observed that he enjoys watching water as it comes out of the tap. Lydia meets with Terrance's family, including his grandmother who takes care of him after school. Together, they determine that learning to brush his teeth independently is a skill that is important to Terrance and his family. His mother is concerned because his other brothers and sisters have had dental problems in the past, and she wants him to have healthy teeth. Lydia discusses with them the challenges that are specific to Terrance, and they remind her that he doesn't mind putting things in his mouth, but he does get upset when something is on his tongue. Lydia and her colleague, Darla, find out what brand of toothpaste the family uses at home and the colour and size of Terrance's toothbrush.

> **VOCABULARY WORDS TO USE WHEN TEACHING TERRANCE TO BRUSH HIS TEETH**
>
> toothbrush
> toothpaste
> lid (top for toothpaste)*
> inside
> outside
> rinse
> teeth
> mouth
> top
> bottom
>
> * Lydia and Darla decide not to use the word cap for the top of the toothpaste, because they know that Terrance is very literal and may be confused because he uses the word cap for the hat he wears on his head.

After the meeting is over and the family has left, Lydia and Darla gather the materials they will need to begin teaching the new skill to Terrance. They decide they will need a toothbrush (just like the one he uses at home), toothpaste (the same brand and flavour used at home) and a plastic cup. They decide they will start teaching Terrance to brush his teeth the following day after the morning snack, and make a list of the vocabulary they will use while they are teaching him this skill (see box at left).

After reviewing the word list, the teachers decide that Terrance will need to review the concepts of *inside, outside, top* and *bottom*, before they start teaching him the steps he needs to take to learn to brush his teeth independently. Next, they write down all the steps Terrance will need to follow to do the task successfully.

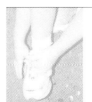

The tooth brushing task analysis includes:

1. Tell Terrance it is time to brush his teeth.
2. Walk into the bathroom with Terrance.
3. Turn on the tap.
4. Run water over the toothbrush.
5. Pick up the toothpaste and open the lid.
6. Put a small amount of toothpaste on the toothbrush.
7. Set the toothbrush down, being careful not to let the toothpaste touch any unclean surfaces.
8. Put the lid on the toothpaste.
9. Pick up the toothbrush and lift it to his mouth.
10. Brush his front teeth.
11. Brush his back teeth.
12. Brush the teeth on top of his mouth.
13. Brush the teeth at the bottom of his mouth.
14. Spit out the toothpaste and turn on the water to rinse it down the drain.
15. Put the toothbrush down.
16. Pick up the glass of water.
17. Rinse the inside of his mouth and spit out the water.
18. Clean the toothbrush.
19. Wipe his mouth with a clean tissue or towel.

Lydia and Darla walked through each step several times and practised modelling it for Terrance. They simplified the list by coming up with a picture schedule. The following day, they showed the picture schedule to Terrance and practised each step together.

The hardest part for Terrance was learning to turn off the water after he had rinsed the sink. However, with practice, he learned to stop watching the water go down the drain and return his attention to finishing the sequence. After two months, he could brush his teeth independently with only minimal assistance from an adult.

Terrance became so familiar with the process of brushing his teeth that he learned to complete each step with only minimal assistance. To help him remember the parts that were most difficult, his teachers held up a picture from his picture schedule to remind him.

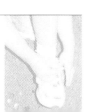

Communicating a need to go to the toilet

This strategy is one of three that can be used to help the child become toilet trained. This strategy is not effective after the child has already had an accident.

What to do

1. Begin by learning the Makaton sign for *toilet*. This is a very simple sign to learn. Make a fist extending the third finger to a pointing gesture and move the hand up and down on your chest. Use this sign with all the children. It is very effective, quickly learned and alleviates children asking aloud to go to the toilet.

2. Once you have learned the sign, begin to use it every time the child goes to the toilet. Make the sign and say, '_____, you need to go to the toilet.'

3. Remember that when a child is first learning a new sign, his attempt to make the sign may be similar but not exactly like the one you want him to use. This is called *approximation*. It is okay for the child to approximate a sign. However, continue to model for him how to make it correctly.

4. Meet with the child's family and encourage them to use the sign with him as well, even if the child is verbal or uses pictures to communicate. Using this sign can be very effective in his overall toilet-training routine.

Helpful hints

◆ A sign is more effective than asking the child to use a picture card because when children with autism need to go to the toilet, they usually need to go immediately; waiting could cause an unwanted accident.

◆ Teach the sign to everyone who works with the child so that they can also use it with him and with all children in the setting.

◆ For Makaton sign resources, contact the charity www.makaton.org.

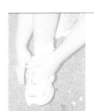

Making toileting work

Start working on toileting skills after you have met with the parents and determined that this is a priority for both the parents and the child. Do not use this strategy when the child has already had an accident or if the child consistently refuses to use the toilet.

What to do

1. Make a list of words that will be used: *potty, toilet, loo, wee, poo, paper, flush* and so on. Make sure the words you use are the same words that are used at home. For example, if you say, 'Do you need to go the toilet?' and at home Mum says, 'Do you need to go to the loo?' then the child will become confused. Talk to the family and decide what words will be used for urinate and defecate. It is not a good idea to use the terms 'number 1' and 'number 2', as these are too abstract.

2. Brainstorm ideas and gather materials that will help the child be successful. For example, a child with tactile sensitivity will need to use very soft toilet paper. Keep in mind that once the child learns the routine, she will need to practise going to the toilet in both familiar and unfamiliar settings.

3. Make going to the toilet a part of the regular everyday routine. Include a picture on the daily picture schedule. Later, after the child learns to associate the picture with going to the toilet, she can learn to walk to the picture and point when she needs to go.

4. Write out each step of the process for yourself. These notes are for you. So, be specific and detailed. Make a list of what will happen first, second and so on.

5. Make a picture schedule for going to the toilet. Use pictures that are very specific and easily understood. Line drawings often work better than detailed colour pictures.

6. Go over the picture schedule with the child before going to the bathroom. Make a game out of the activity. Talk about what happens first, what happens second and so on.

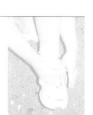

7. Take the child to the toilet and go through each step with her. It may be necessary for you to model for her what to do, such as pulling up her pants after she finishes or drying her hands after she washes them.

8. Encourage the child to be as independent as possible; remember that success requires consistency, patience and practice.

9. Don't forget to praise the child for any successful attempt. Remember, the goal is for the child to learn to use the toilet independently. Communicating that she needs to go is a separate goal.

Helpful hints

- Encouraging the child to drink water or other liquid prior to practising this routine is often helpful.
- Initially, practise with the child when other children are not present.
- Anticipate that children with autism may have additional issues with the toilet, such as fear of sitting on the toilet, avoidance of touching toilet paper or of wiping themselves, a need to flush over and over, and a resistance to change, which may include a resistance to giving up wearing a nappy.
- Because children with autism don't always adapt well to new settings, anticipate that a child who is perfectly trained to use the toilet in familiar places may hesitate to use unfamiliar toilets.

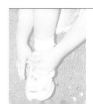

Bathroom detective: when a child gets upset in the toilet

Use this strategy when the child has had some success with independent toilet use and suddenly becomes resistant to using the toilet.

What to do

1. Try to determine the root cause of the toilet problem. Start by looking for the obvious. Knowing that children with autism require very set routines, ask yourself the following question: What was different today? Perhaps a different person took the child to the toilet or perhaps, rather than being the only child in the toilet, there were several other children present.

2. Look at other factors as well. Did you insist the child go when he was involved in a favourite activity in the classroom? Did you make him go at a time that was different from when you asked him to go yesterday?

3. Immediately following the incident, take a trip to the toilet yourself to see if you can work out what might have changed. Use the toilet checklist to help you.

4. If you did not take the child to the toilet, speak to the person who did. Explain to that person that you are not criticising or blaming him for the child's refusal to go. You just need information to help you determine what went wrong.

5. Accept the fact that you may never really know what has gone wrong, and try again later.

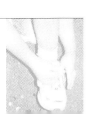

Toilet checklist

Questions	Comments
Look around the toilet. Does it look physically the same as it did before? Even a small change such as a new colour or new sign can be distracting.	
Does the child have a certain cubicle that he prefers? If so, was it available?	
Is the toilet paper the same as the day before? If not, what is different about it?	
Is there an unfamiliar or new smell in the toilet? Even the addition of a new air freshener can be upsetting for a child with autism.	
Can you see anything else that may be different from when the child previously used the toilet?	

Helpful hints

- If the child continues to be resistant, check with his parents to see if he is having a problem at home as well.
- The problem may be unrelated to the toilet itself; the child may not feel well or may be constipated.

Learning to put on socks/shoes

To put on socks and shoes independently with minimal assistance or prompting.

What to do

1. Make a list of the steps that the child needs to follow to put on his socks and shoes. Determine if you are going to teach him to put on both socks, then both shoes, or if you are going to complete putting the sock and shoe on one foot before attempting the other one.
2. Make a task analysis of each step the child will need to follow.
3. See if the child will let you model each step for him, using your own socks and shoes.
4. Ask him to watch you. Then, he should try it himself.
5. Praise him for attempting to put on his own socks and shoes.
6. Make a series of three or four picture cards to help remind him of the correct sequence in the activity. Most children have shoes that are attached with Velcro, so tying shoe laces should not be an issue.
7. If the child appears to be sensitive about the socks or gets anxious, check and make sure they are on his feet properly. Children with autism often tend to be very sensitive when material is scratchy or does not fit properly.

Helpful hints

◆ Don't be overly concerned if the child refuses to take off his shoes. Some children with autism do not like to have their feet exposed to the air, or may be sensitive to having their feet touched.
◆ Play games with several children where everyone takes off their shoes and socks, and then puts them back on in time to music.
◆ Be flexible. If the child doesn't want to put on his shoes, but puts on his socks that's fine. See if he will let you help him.
◆ If the child continues to have difficulty, try a process called *reverse or backward chaining*. This means you break down the steps of the task and learn them in reverse order, last step first. This gives the child a sense of success every time they work on the task.

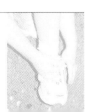

Mealtime fun!

To make mealtime an enjoyable experience for the child and his peers.

What to do

1. Observe the child during a meal, using the mealtime/snack observation checklist on page 65. Pay close attention to other factors, such as whether he prefers to sit beside the same peer every day, whether he eats more consistently when food is presented on a plate with divided compartments, and whether he asks for more if he wants more.

2. With the checklist as a guide, look at the child's preferences when planning the mealtime routine.

3. If you leave your play area for meals, be sure to tell the child

Learning to eat with a fork is not easy.

a few minutes early to allow him to get ready for meals. Go to the picture schedule or visual timetable and point to the picture that shows eating.

4. As children with autism generally prefer structure and routine, it helps if the child has an assigned seat for mealtimes. Be aware of sensory issues and distractions – buzzing lights, shadows, leaves fluttering on trees outside and so on.

5. For family-style eating, model for the child how to ask for more. If the child is non verbal, teach him the Makaton sign for 'more' (see opposite).

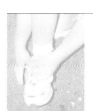

6. Make a placemat using the child's favourite colour. The mat can be made of cardboard or construction paper and laminated. Draw on the placemat where each utensil will be placed – draw a large circle for the child's plate and a smaller one for his cup.
7. In the home corner encourage the child to role play eating a pretend meal and try some simple role play, such as giving a doll a drink and so on.
8. Encourage the child to be as independent as possible at mealtimes, but recognise that children with autism often experience distress over eating and may refuse to eat or refuse to try new foods.

Helpful hints

- Don't force the child to try new foods.
- If possible, reduce the light level and use indirect lighting during mealtimes.
- Spills are a natural part of eating. If the child spills something and gets upset, talk quietly and assure him that everything is just fine.
- Sometimes, children with autism get so upset that they throw food or plates on the floor. When this happens, ask the child if he has finished eating and redirect him while you clean up the spill.
- If the child gets up and leaves the table, smile at the other children and praise them for sitting and eating with their friends. Don't try to force the child to return to the table.
- Make mealtimes as relaxing as possible. Play soft music or talk quietly with the children while they eat.

Mealtime/snack observation checklist

Observe the child periodically. Use this checklist to help monitor the progress of the child. If the child is inconsistent in a specific area, tick the box that says 'sometimes'. Write any comments that will help you in the box beside each question.

Ask yourself...	Yes	No	Some-times	Comments
Does the child sit in the same chair during meals?				
Does the child sit by the same person each time he eats?				
Does the child use utensils when he eats? If so, which ones?				
Will the child let one food touch another?				
Does the child eat a variety of foods?				
Will the child try new foods?				
Does the child seem to have a mealtime ritual? (Folding napkin a certain way, arranging his plate a certain way and so on)				
How does the child let you know if he wants more?				
How does the child let you know if he has finished?				

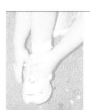

Hand washing

To establish a routine where the child independently washes her hands.

What to do

1. Picture sequence cards are always helpful, but this strategy depends on modelling what you want the child to do.
2. Walk with the child to the sink.
3. Tell her that you are going to play a game where you do something and then she does the same thing.
4. Say, 'First, we turn on the water.' Turn on the water. (Wait to see if the child turns on her tap, too.)
5. Say, 'Now, we get some soap.' Put some soap on your hands. (Wait to see if the child puts soap on her hands.)
6. Say, 'Next, we put our hands under the water.' Put your hands under the water, and wait to see if the child does the same thing.
7. Say, 'Now, we rub our hands together and count to 10.' Rub soap on your hands and count to 10.
8. Say, 'Next, we rinse the soap off our hands.' (Wait to see if the child rinses her hands. If she does not, repeat the instructions.)
9. Say, 'Finally, we dry our hands.' Reach for a paper towel and dry your hands.
10. Say, 'Now, we put the towel into the trash.'

Helpful hints

- If the child refuses to participate in the activity, help her gradually to learn to accept the routine by partially participating such as doing only one or two steps before trying the whole routine independently.
- Remember, if the child is hesitant or resistant to any part of this routine, try to determine the cause. Maybe the towels are too rough or the water is too hot or too cold.
- Try to use the same words and follow the same procedure each time you practise the routine.
- After the child has learned the routine, see if she can do it independently.

Crossing the road

This strategy begins to develop awareness of road safety.

What to do

1. Even though an adult will probably be present when a child crosses the road, it is still important that he learns what to do.

2. Try to use this strategy when you are crossing a real road. Practise outside, so that the child learns to associate this strategy with crossing a real road.

3. Teach the child the following song, sung to the tune of 'Three Blind Mice'.

   Stop, look and listen,
   Stop, look and listen,
   When you cross the road,
   When you cross the road.
   Look to the left and then to the right.
   Look to the left and then to the right.
   Remember, every time you cross the road to
   Stop, look and listen,
   Stop, look and listen.

4. Practise the song several times, crossing the road as you sing.

Helpful hints

◆ Although children with autism don't role-play well, try singing the song and role-play crossing the road in your classroom.

◆ Remember to sing the song every time you cross the road with the child.

◆ Share the song with the child's family and other caregivers and encourage them to sing the song as they cross the road with the child, as well.

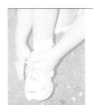

Key terms

Approximation: An inexact representation of a skill or a word that is still close enough to be useful. Can be seen as an 'emerging' skill.

Functional skills: Everyday skills that the child will use to be more independent, sometimes called self-help, life skills or independent living skills. Functional skills are the skills a child will use throughout his life, such as brushing his teeth, going to the toilet and taking a bath.

Hyper-sensitivity: Overly sensitive to something, the state of being overly stimulated by the environment.

Backward or reverse chaining: Breaking down a task or skill into small achievable steps and reaching them in reverse order, last step first. This allows the child to have success and complete the task each time they practise the skill.

Task analysis: The breaking down of a skill into small steps; step-by-step guide.

CHAPTER 5

Misbehaviour or missed communication:

Managing the behaviours of children with autism

How will I ever understand the unusual behaviours of children with autism?

Children with autism often have behavioural characteristics that are not typically seen in other children of the same age, such as hand flapping or screaming out loud. Some children with autism will behave like their typically developing peers, but that behaviour may be more intense or prolonged, as when a three-year-old throws a tantrum. Instead of lasting only a few minutes, it may last much longer. A challenging behaviour is defined as any action where the child deliberately hurts himself, injures others and/or causes damage to his environment. Such behaviour may socially isolate the child and further limit how others want to interact with him.

Crying can be a way to avoid something.

Challenging behaviour may be the result of a child who is:

- frustrated or confused by a new situation or activity
- afraid of something
- experiencing a panic or anxiety attack
- extremely frustrated and responds by hurting herself or a classmate
- very impulsive and can't seem to control his desire to do something
- attached to an inanimate object
- upset because a ritual has been interrupted
- stopped from doing something that is comforting to her.

Some strategies for dealing with challenging behaviours

In general, a typical response to a specific behaviour is that the child acts and the adult reacts. When a child behaves a certain way, such as hitting another child or throwing an object, the practitioner must immediately determine an effective way of addressing the situation (react). This 'action-reaction' cycle is rarely effective in stopping the disruptive behaviour of a child with autism. In fact, under some circumstances, it may make the behaviour worse.

For example, some conventional adult reactions to challenging behaviour may include the following:

> The reason that these conventional action-reaction cycles are not always effective for children with autism is that the strategies focus on the behaviour itself and not the reason behind the behaviour. When working with children with autism, it is important to look at both the form (what the child is doing) and the function (why the child is doing it).

- Trying to stop the child's challenging behaviour by praising when he is not doing the challenging behaviour.
- You might enforce a natural consequence for a specific action, such as when a child throws a block. The natural consequence might be that he cannot play with blocks again for a given period.
- After the behaviour has occurred, the key person may try to talk to the child and explain why that specific behaviour is not acceptable.
- An attempt may be made to redirect the child away from what is upsetting her, in an effort to refocus her attention on something new or novel.

What is meant by form and function?

The form is the way the child behaves. For example, if Kara throws a book, the *form* of the behaviour is throwing. When Michael hits himself repeatedly, the form of the behaviour is self-injurious or hitting. The form of the behaviour tells us what the child is doing; it does not tell us why he is doing it.

Why a child behaves in a certain way can be more important than how she behaves. Understanding why helps practitioners plan strategies that can often prevent the behaviour from happening. The motivation (why) behind something the child does is called the *function* of the behaviour. It is the

reason or the purpose that the behaviour serves. For example, Kara may be throwing the book because she is frustrated and overwhelmed by all the noise in the room. Michael may be hitting himself because the teacher has told him it is time to stop an activity that he enjoys.

Why a child behaves a certain way can be more important than how she behaves. Understanding why helps with planning strategies that can often prevent the behaviour from happening.

There are two basic functions or reasons behind challenging behaviours. The child either wants to avoid or escape from someone or something, or wants access to something. In other words, he wants an object or an outcome and he does not have the communication skills to ask for it.

How can I determine the function or reason for a child's behaviour?

The best way to understand why a child behaves in a certain way is to examine what is going on just before or just after the behaviour occurs. This process is called a functional assessment and determines the relationship between events in a child's environment and the occurrence of challenging behaviours. This process involves:

- identifying and defining the challenging behaviour
- identifying the events and circumstances that are happening or not happening when the child is behaving in a certain way
- determining the social reason behind the challenging behaviour.

For example, Marissa goes outside and stands watching while two children throw a ball back and forth. They put down the ball and go to the swings. Marissa starts to scream and hit herself. Watching the children throw the ball was enjoyable for Marissa. When they stopped, she was angry because she wanted to continue watching them throw the ball. In this example, the screaming was the *form* (type of behaviour) and the children stopping was the *function* (reason behind the behaviour). The event that she enjoyed (watching the children play ball) was taken away from her, so she screamed as a way of protesting.

The events that relate to a behaviour can often help determine why the behaviour occurs. These are sometimes called *setting events* – conditions

that occur at the same time as a challenging behaviour occurs. These setting events often increase the likelihood that a challenging behaviour may occur. Knowing what events or conditions may cause a child to behave in a certain way helps reduce or stop a challenging behaviour before it starts. The best intervention is prevention!

The following are examples of some setting events:

Waiting for a turn is not easy.

- staff changes or a key person's absence
- sleep (too much or too little)
- illness (even though children with autism may not express symptoms of feeling unwell in the same way as other children)
- situations that are new or demanding for the child
- an environment that is chaotic and disorganised
- disruptions in the regular routine of the day, such as a fire drill or a field trip
- changes in temperature (room temperature and weather) or light intensity
- waiting a long time for something she wants
- waiting too long to eat or sleep
- a preferred toy or item placed somewhere different in the setting.

While you may never completely be able to stop a child with autism from behaving in a certain way, you may greatly be able to reduce the challenging behaviours by creating an environment that is proactive (preventative) rather than one that is reactive (only responds after the child misbehaves).

When planning for a positive environment, look at the following:

The organisation of the setting, group size and so on: Look at appropriate options for the child. Sometimes, an environment or situation can be too stressful. The child may need a more or less structured setting. There may be too many children in the setting or the activity level may be too intense. The session may be too long for the child or she may need to come to school later in the day or leave earlier in the afternoon.

Curriculum: Developmentally appropriate practice in early childhood involves learning how to interact and get along with others. Interaction with others involves using social skills. Other children may struggle with a child with poor social skills. When peers socially reject a child, it reduces the natural opportunities for a child to learn social skills with peers and may worsen her behaviour problems.

Select resources that encourage interaction.

Resources: Resources can make it easier for a child to respond in a more positive manner. Select resources that encourage interaction (for example, blocks, a ball or a swing) and lessen the possibility of the child's reacting in a negative manner. Make sure there are enough resources and that the child does not have to wait too long for his turn.

Keep rules simple: Avoid too many rules or rules that are vague and abstract. Display them where all of the children can see them and refer to them often. Picture representations of the rules will probably help all children, including children with autism, to learn and keep the boundaries in mind.

The keys to a child with autism being successful in an early years setting include:

- a physical environment that promotes interaction and that is neither too stimulating nor too overwhelming for the child
- rules that guide behaviour and are simple and concrete
- resources that encourage persistence and attention
- routines that are easily followed and understood
- transitions that are simple and clear.

Make consequences natural and be consistent! Children with autism become confused when there are inconsistencies in how and when things happen.

How do I know what procedure to use?

What strategy you use depends on several factors. First, you must select a behaviour that both you and the child's family wish to change. Second, you must decide if the function of the challenging behaviour (either to escape/avoid or gain access) is acceptable. For example, if Meleka throws a tantrum

every time you ask her to stop working in the literacy area and join circle time, you might decide that you can honour her reason (not wanting to stop) and show her how to let you know that she wants more time before coming to the circle. When a child learns to replace a negative behaviour with a more acceptable behaviour, such as letting you know she needs more time, you are teaching her to use a communicative replacement.

A communicative replacement – 'more'.

A *communicative replacement* is a form of communication or a message that the child gives you to replace the behaviour. Let's look at an example of using a communicative replacement in this situation. You may help Meleka know when it is time to make a transition by giving her an unbreakable sand timer and telling her that when the sand runs out, it will be time to leave the literacy area and come to the large group circle. She will have a clear visual signal with the sand timer and knowing that there will be a given time to go to the circle may lessen her stress about it.

There may be some functions you cannot honour. For example, if Micah screams and hits himself every time you ask him to eat something, then you might decide that the function or reason for his behaviour is to escape eating his lunch. You cannot honour this because you know that he has to eat lunch at school. In this instance, use a strategy that would help Micah control his behaviour, but not allow him to escape eating. For example, let him listen to his favourite music while he eats or allow him to make choices about what he eats. He might prefer to eat alone with headphones on; while this does little to encourage socialisation, it does disrupt the cycle of hitting himself at lunch time. In other words, the procedure or strategy you select depends on whether you can honour or allow the reason behind the child's behaviour.

Components of a functional assessment

- Identify and define the challenging behaviour.
- Identify the events and circumstances that are happening or not happening when the child is behaving in a certain way.
- Determine the social reason behind the challenging behaviour.

Space invaders!

To help the child learn to signal when someone is too close to him and he feels threatened by their proximity.

What to do

1. Work with the child to make a picture of an alien. Glue or tape the alien picture on to a lolly stick, making a stick puppet. An alternative to this would be a hand puppet made from a sock.

2. Explain that whenever another child gets too close, the child with autism can either raise his stick puppet or put the hand puppet on his hand.

3. Ask for a peer volunteer and model how to use the hand puppet so that all the children in the room understand that when the child with autism raises his puppet he is trying to say, 'You are standing too close to me!'

4. Explain that the child is saying that he wants the invader to step back before trying to talk or play with him.

5. Ask for some volunteers and practise the activity together.

6. Place the puppet in a location where the child with autism has easy access to it.

7. Remember to reward the child verbally when he attempts to use this strategy instead of behaving in an inappropriate manner.

Helpful hints

◆ Sometimes children with autism need extra practice before they can use a strategy consistently across situations.

◆ Play a game with this strategy so all the children in the class know how and why the child uses his puppet.

Misbehaviour or missed communication   75

Distract and redirect

Try this when you feel that the child is becoming upset or spending too much time fixating on a particular object or activity.

Redirect to a favourite activity.

What to do

1. Walk up to the child and start to hum his favourite song ('Wheels on the Bus', 'Incey Wincey Spider' or 'Tommy Thumb'). This will get his attention in a way that does not alarm or upset him.
2. Touch the item or point to the place or item that you wish to redirect the child towards.
3. Look at the child, then look at the item.
4. Gently guide him towards the new object or activity. If he does not follow you, gently reach out and take his elbow or hand.
5. Walk slowly together towards the object.
6. Sit down with the child and hand him the object.
7. Smile at him and stay for a few minutes while he explores the new object.

Helpful hints

◆ Children with autism often do not like to be redirected from an activity or object that they are involved with. Try standing beside the child and humming for a few minutes before you start redirecting him to the new activity.

Waiting

This strategy can be used when the child is waiting in line for something. It works best with small groups of children.

What to do

1. Give the child something to do with her hands while she waits. A squishy toy or a soft squeezable object works best.
2. Play music that is soft and enjoyable so all the children have something to listen to when they are waiting for a turn.
3. If the activity is one that can be counted, such as each child gets two goes at throwing a beanbag into a box, ask the child with autism to help you count as each child takes a turn.
4. When you are beginning to teach this strategy, let the child go second or third. Waiting too long the first few times can cause her to be too anxious.
5. Later, when the child has learned to wait, place her further back in the line.
6. Verbally praise the child for waiting her turn.

Helpful hints

- If you play music, teach the child a few body movements that she can do while waiting.
- As each child steps forward to take a turn, verbally announce who will be next. For example, 'After Dean finishes it will be Althea's turn.'
- Try using first–then cards, which show what a child must do *first*, before *then* getting to do a preferred activity.

Change in routine

To help the child accept a change in the daily routine without becoming upset or displaying disruptive behaviour.

What to do

1. Begin by making some planned changes in a child's schedule, to give him (and you) opportunities to learn how to deal with such changes.
2. Walk with the child to where his daily schedule or visual timetable is displayed. It is a good idea to attach the cards to the display board or wall with Velcro so that you can change them easily.
3. Talk about the timetable and what will happen next. Show him the new card that you have made and describe what the card represents. For example, 'Today we are having a special music concert after storytime. I made a picture for you.' Show the picture to the child.

4. Remove the card that the new picture will replace and attach the picture to the schedule.
5. Talk about the change in schedule. Just before it is time for the concert, show the card that represents the concert to the child.
6. In order for the child to discriminate occasional activities from regular routine activities, try making the special activity card on a different coloured background such as yellow or pale orange. Be consistent. Every time there is a new occasional activity, depict it on the same colour. In time, the child will come to identify that all activities pictured on that colour card will be special or occasional in nature.

Hands at home

To help the child keep her hands at her sides, therefore reducing stereotypical behaviours such as hand flapping and hand wringing.

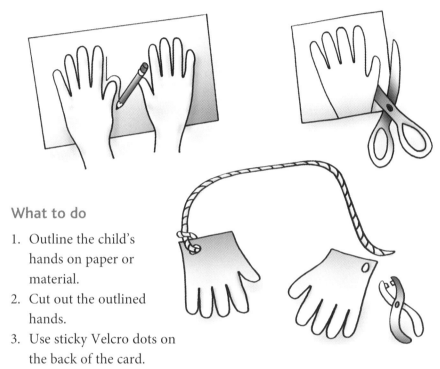

What to do

1. Outline the child's hands on paper or material.
2. Cut out the outlined hands.
3. Use sticky Velcro dots on the back of the card.
4. Place the hand shapes on a table or in the child's lap.
5. Coach the child so that when you say, 'Hands at home', she knows to place her hands on the cutout hands.

Helpful hints

◆ Remember that many children with autism have difficulty touching certain textures and materials. Be sure to use paper or material that is of a colour and texture that the child can enjoy.

Today, I feel...

This strategy should be enjoyable for the child so that she learns to express how she is feeling. It will help the child learn to communicate her emotional state.

What to do

1. Make a set of feeling cards. Begin with two: *happy* and *sad*. Later, you might add other cards such as *cross, surprised* and so on.
2. Talk about each card. Identify the emotion for the child. Hold up the card with the happy picture photograph or symbol and say, 'This card shows a feeling. This is happy.'
3. Show the child the card that describes what you say. For example, say, 'It makes me happy when I see children play.' Then, hold up or point to the card showing happy.
4. Repeat the same activity using sad. Say, 'It makes me sad when _____.' Hold up or point to the card showing sad.
5. Ask the child a question to see if she can point to the card that best describes how she feels. For example, 'How does it make you feel when you fall down?' Then, after waiting for a response, point to the picture of sad.
6. Throughout the day, use the cards and ask the child a question. If she points to the card, verbally respond with, 'Thank you for telling me how you feel.'
7. Use the cards until the child understands that the cards describe an emotion. It may take several days or weeks. Mount the cards near the child's picture schedule and encourage her to point to them to tell you how she is feeling.

Helpful hints

◆ Mount the cards in several places, so the child will have access to them.
◆ Add other cards to the feelings picture cards.
◆ After the child is familiar with the activity, use them when she is just starting to get upset about something – before she begins to behave inappropriately.

Key terms

Challenging behaviour: A problem behaviour defined as any action where the child deliberately hurts himself, injures others and/or causes damage to his environment.

Communicative replacement: A form of communication or a message that the child gives to you that replaces the behaviour.

Form: The way a child behaves.

Function: The reason why something happens. The function of a behaviour is the reason behind the behaviour.

Functional assessment: An evaluation designed to determine the relationship between events in a child's environment and the occurrence of challenging behaviours.

Natural consequence: The logical result of an action.

Proactive: A procedure or action that happens before a problem occurs and is designed to prevent the behaviour from occurring.

Setting event: Conditions that occur at the same time as a challenging behaviour occurs.

CHAPTER 6

Signs, symbols and language:
Helping a child to communicate

Using communication in a social setting

What exactly is communication?

For the purposes of this book, we will define communication as an interaction between two or more people where information is exchanged. In other words, when one person sends a message to another person, we say they are communicating. Three aspects of communication (see table below) determine how well a child learns to communicate: form, function and content.

How does communication differ in children with autism in the early years?

Language disorders are often widely accepted as typical of children with autism. In fact, it may be the most noticed characteristic. A language disorder may be defined as a deficit in using words or vocabulary. It can also involve how a child understands language and uses it in social settings. For

Aspects of communication

Communication	Definition	Example
Form	A way to communicate	Crying, talking, gestures, sign language, pointing to picture cards
Function	A reason to communicate	Hungry, want something, need something or someone, need attention, making a choice
Content	Purpose of communication	The child needs experiences and opportunities to explore, so that he will have something to communicate about

children with autism, a pragmatic language delay is often seen. Pragmatic language involves using language in a social setting. For example, knowing what is appropriate to say, when to say it and the general give-and-take nature of a friendly conversation. Because autism is a spectrum ranging from severe to very mild, children with autism will have communication abilities that range from not talking at all (non verbal) to being able to communicate effectively. Often, children with autism who talk will appear to use words and speech in a way that is not meaningful or less functional than their peers.

What do we mean by communication that is not meaningful?

Non-functional communication is speech that is understood and spoken clearly but has no relevance to the interaction that is taking place. For example, four-year-old Evan knows how to talk and does so frequently, but when you ask him to go outside, he simply says, 'Bottom of the ninth and the bases are loaded.' Evan is communicating. In fact, he is answering her question. Unfortunately, he is answering it in a non-functional manner. However, sometimes what sounds like non-functional communication can, with careful observation, be the child's way of answering in a way that makes sense to him. In other words, there are times when non-functional communication from an adult's perspective is functional for the child. What Evan could really mean is, 'Going outside is very stressful.'

How can non-functional communication be functional for the child?

To answer this question, let's examine how James answers questions. He is five, knows about colours, and can name and describe each of them. However, when asked, 'James, what is your favourite colour?' he replies, 'Lemon yellow.' On the other hand, when asked, 'Would you like to go to the brick activity?' he replies 'Crimson red.' It appears that he is answering the first question appropriately or functionally, while his answer to the second question is non-functional and not appropriate.

James' key person has been observing his communication for some time and has determined that every time James responds with 'crimson red' it is James' way of saying 'No!' He has also observed that when James means 'yes', he answers with 'sunset orange'. His key person, through observation and experience, has learned to interpret the meaning behind James' non-functional communication. But it does not mean that James' practitioners need to stop encouraging him to answer 'yes' or 'no'. It means that, while he is learning to answer 'yes' and 'no', people around him, at least, know how to interpret the way in which James is currently expressing his wishes and making choices.

Children with autism who have difficulties with functional communication may use echolalia when responding to others. It can be very frustrating for an adult when everything you say is repeated back to you.

What exactly is echolalia?

Echolalia is the echoing and repetition of a phrase or word. This is especially common in some children with autism who do not use speech functionally.

> There are times when a child with echolalia is not even aware he is doing anything out of the ordinary.

Echolalia can be an instant response – meaning that the child will repeat a phrase immediately after it is heard. For example, you say, 'Time for small group' and the child immediately repeats, 'Time for small group'. A child might repeat the phrase multiple times, 'Time for small group, time for small group, time for small group'. Often, echolalia cannot be controlled or stopped on command. There are times when a child with echolalia is not even aware he is doing anything out of the ordinary.

At other times, children use echolalia as a way to communicate intentionally. The repeated phrase has meaning to the child, and they attempt to use the phrase in conversation. For example, when mum asks Bailey about his day at school, Bailey might respond with the phrase 'time for small group', as a way to communicate that he went to group at school.

Delayed echolalia can occur hours, days or weeks after it is first heard. This type of echolalia is unpredictable and may happen because a child hears a phrase he likes. For example, Sam heard the expression, 'Beam me up, Scotty!' from the television series *Star Trek*. He used the expression over and over all day long, much to the frustration of his teacher. However, when

the teacher observed the context or the situations in which he used it most often, she found it was when he was frustrated or when a new activity had been introduced. In his own way, Sam was using the phrase, 'Beam me up, Scotty!' to express his anxiety over the new task. While the expression in itself made no sense to others, for Sam, it had meaning.

Paula Kluth, in her book *You're Going to Love this Kid,* makes several suggestions as to how a person might respond to echolalia. First, she suggests that the listener reassures the child. A teacher might say, 'I think you are trying to tell me _____.' or 'I'm sorry. I don't understand. Are you trying to tell me _____?' The response of the listener is an attempt to show the child that she is listening and encourages the child to keep trying to let her know what he wants.

It may be that some children with echolalia respond better when the person who is talking with them whispers.

Her second strategy is called 'going to the cinema', which means that when a child repeats a phrase from a film or television show, the teacher tries to determine whether the child is using that phrase to communicate a message. Once the practitioner has figured out what the phrase means to the child, a key can be made for others to follow. For example, Sam uses the phrase, 'Beam me up, Scotty!' when he is frightened because to him, it means, 'I'm scared and don't understand what to do next.'

Another technique for handling echolalia is to use it to your benefit. For example, you ask the child, 'Do you want a cookie?' and the child replies, 'Do you want a cookie?' You then say what you want the child to say, 'Yes, I want a cookie.' This allows you to build the relationship between what the child says and what is intended.

Finally, it has been suggested that some children with echolalia respond better when the person who is talking with them whispers. The idea is that the listener becomes occupied with trying to hear the speaker and doesn't respond with echolalia.

Why do children with autism have so much trouble communicating?

Effective communication is more than just sending and receiving messages. It requires that one person, either the sender or the receiver of the message, interacts with the other person. Actually, for the interaction to be successful, the other person must reciprocate in some way. In initiating an exchange of a message or information, the sender must be willing to approach the person she will be communicating with. Although the child with autism may be able to answer a direct question or make a statement about what she wants, starting a conversation is especially difficult. In fact, a child with autism will more likely initiate a communication when she wants or needs something. It is less likely she will initiate communication simply for the sake of a social interaction.

It is generally agreed that communication can be divided into expressive and receptive. Expressive communication has to do with how the child inputs his message to the person receiving it. In other words, how he uses communication to express himself. Receptive communication is how the child receives messages or information from others. Speech and language therapists and other experts in the field of communication have always believed that a child can receive messages much earlier than he can generate them. Therefore, a child's receptive language generally develops before his expressive language.

Although the child with autism may be able to answer a direct question or make a statement about what she wants, starting a conversation is especially difficult.

Speech and language therapists are excellent resources for helping determine not only how and why a child communicates, but what can be done to enhance his communication. For a child to communicate effectively, he must be able to communicate on purpose. This is called intentional communication.

What is intentional communication?

Intentional communication is communication that happens for a reason. It is purposeful. For example, when babies are first beginning to experiment with sound, they may repeat the same sounds over and over again. For example, a baby may say 'ba-ba-boo-boo-ba-ba-boo-boo' repeatedly. This experiment with sound is probably pre-intentional communication; she is most likely experimenting with sound and enjoys the way it feels to say it over and over again.

However, if when she says, 'ba-ba-boo-boo-ba-ba-boo-boo' and her mother or caregiver comes over to the cot and says, 'Oh, you want your

ba-ba?' and gets the child a favourite toy, the child soon learns that whenever she says, 'ba-ba-boo-boo-ba-ba-boo-boo' a friendly face appears and gives her some attention. Therefore, what may start out as pre-intentional communication can quickly become intentional.

Let's look at another example. As a baby starts to develop her gross motor skills, she may stretch out her arms towards the sky. If she does this and an

Asking a friend to play by using a picture

adult interprets this gesture as meaning the baby wants to be picked up, the behaviour will eventually become intentional on the part of the baby.

These examples illustrate the importance of responding to any attempt by the child to communicate, whether or not the attempt is intentional. This is especially true of children with autism who often do not attempt to communicate intentionally. Intentional communication is quite different, however, from echolalia.

How do I start helping a child communicate?

The best place to start is by observing the child until you have determined which methods or actions he uses to communicate and under what conditions he is most likely to communicate. In general terms, a child will communicate when:

- he is able to attend to what is being said
- he is able to understand what is said by others
- he experiences the responsiveness of others to his attempts at communication
- he has a reason to communicate.

It is also important to find out what motivates a child. Look for reasons why he might or might not communicate. Learn to recognise that children with autism do not communicate in the same way as their peers. For example, if Kerry throws down her food when the teacher places it in front of her, she may be communicating that she does not want to eat. In this

case, it would be helpful for everyone involved to work together to figure out an alternative way for her to communicate that she is not hungry. It will be necessary for all who work with the child to determine her stage of communication. Trying to force a child to communicate before she is ready not only frustrates the child, but could also delay her progress.

What do we mean by stages of communication?

The various stages of communication have been given a variety of names and defined in many different ways. For the purposes of this book, only those stages that pre-school children might experience will be discussed. A speech and language therapist can help you learn more about the traditional developmental stages of communication. The stages that most pre-school children will experience have been condensed for this book and include:

- ◆ 'It's all about me' – egocentric stage
- ◆ 'I want it' – requesting stage
- ◆ Actions and reactions – emerging communication stage
- ◆ Two-way street – reciprocal communication stage.

Egocentric stage

The 'It's all about me' (egocentric) stage usually occurs in typically developing children when they are around two years old. Because children with autism may be delayed in their overall development, it is not uncommon for a child with autism to communicate in this stage when she arrives in your pre-school setting. Children in the egocentric stage might:

- ◆ reach their hands out to indicate 'I want'
- ◆ scream or cry when they don't get something they want
- ◆ smile or laugh when someone looks at them
- ◆ be very shy around strangers
- ◆ not interact with other children, but interact with adults who are familiar to them
- ◆ experiment with how language sounds and say phrases repeatedly.

Requesting stage

The 'I want it' (requesting) stage occurs as the child learns cause and effect. He begins to understand that what he says or does has an effect on people or on his environment. During this stage, a child starts to see communication as a means to get what he wants.

Children in the requesting stage might:

♦ grab your hand and pull you towards something they want
♦ say a few basic words
♦ move their bodies when you are interacting with them to communicate 'I want more'
♦ begin to sign the word 'more', by putting their hands together
♦ approximate words or attempt a few new words.

Emerging communication stage

The child who functions in the emerging communication stage is beginning to use communication in a more functional manner. She is starting to understand that she can repeat the same action, gesture or word and it gets the same result. Children in this stage will put two words together and seem to enjoy repeating what they have just heard. The communication

Communicating involves a partner.

interactions that occur with the child are much longer and more sustained than in the previous stages.

Children in the emerging communication stage might:

♦ take turns
♦ understand the names of those familiar to them
♦ repeat what they have just heard
♦ use gestures more consistently, such as shaking their heads 'no'
♦ answer simple questions
♦ ask for something or request that you continue something
♦ use words or signs in a more meaningful way.

Reciprocal communication stage

The 'two-way street' (reciprocal communication) stage is characterised by more direct communication with a partner. Often, children in this stage are more prone to communicate with an adult than with a peer. While children with autism continue to have difficulty with initiating or beginning conversations with peers, children at this stage may participate in a conversation if they have a strong need or a motivation to get something from the other child.

Children with autism rarely initiate spontaneous communication. If the child communicates, she still needs for conversations to be very concrete and literal. Steven Shore, a man with autism, recalls when he was a child, a peer said to him, 'I feel like a pizza.' Steven did not respond to the peer because he had no idea how a 'pizza feels' – after all, pizzas don't have feelings. Children in this stage of communication may have difficulty with social cues, new social situations and understanding the abstracts of language, such as jokes. They also have difficulty understanding when someone is teasing them or making light of something. Children in the reciprocal communication stage might:

◆ intentionally use words to greet, ask for something, protest about something, ask questions and comment about something
◆ express ideas and feelings that are relevant to them
◆ have short conversations (although children with autism will always be more easily distracted than their peers)
◆ repeat something, if they think the listener does not understand
◆ start to use longer sentences with more descriptive words.

How do I set appropriate goals for communication?

It is difficult to know which goals to set when a child is learning to communicate. It is equally challenging to know what to expect from a child with autism, especially at the pre-school level. While each child is unique and will communicate in his own way, there are several general suggestions to think about when setting communication goals.

The ultimate goal for any child is to learn to communicate because it is meaningful to him...to learn to do more than just tell you what he wants and needs...

Communication is most effective when it involves interaction with others. Learning to interact with other people is a life skill that the child can build on and use throughout his life.

In order to communicate effectively, the child must have a reliable form or way to communicate. During the pre-school years, it is important to help the child use a form that will enable him to interact with his peers.

The ultimate goal for any child is to learn to communicate because it is meaningful to him. You want the child with autism to learn to do more than just tell you what he wants and needs; you want him to learn to use communication as a form of self-expression.

In addition to the general guidelines above, the communication goals found in the table below are based on the child's stage of communication.

Communication goals

Stage of communication	Goals
Egocentric	◆ Offer real choices. Encourage the child to show you what he wants by touching, pointing, gesturing or using sign language. ◆ Play simple games that involve taking turns, such as rolling a ball back and forth. Use commentary to describe actions. Say, 'It's my turn' and point to yourself, then say, 'It's your turn' and point to the child. ◆ Consistently respond to every communication attempt, even if it is unintentional. Verbalise what the child is doing.
Requesting	◆ Play a game or start an activity. Then, stop and try to get the child to 'ask for more', either by moving his body or looking at you. ◆ When the child pulls you towards something or points to a desired object, respond. Then, verbalise what he wanted and say the name of the object. ◆ Describe everything the child does. Remember to use simple sentences. ◆ Children with autism often respond poorly to continuous talk. They may be under-responsive to verbal stimuli. Provide a model. Say it from the child's point of view. Wait expectantly, and show rather than say often.
Emerging	◆ Continue to play games that involve taking turns, but also encourage the child to play with or alongside other children. ◆ Provide an exact model of what you want the child to say and do. ◆ Respond to any situations where the child initiates a communication interaction. ◆ Build on the child's expanding vocabulary by providing experiences that will help him develop new words. ◆ If the child is using pictures to communicate, try to encourage him to use words, too.
Reciprocal	◆ Set up situations that encourage conversation. ◆ Throughout all stages, the environment plays a major role in helping children interact. ◆ Play games where you practise the rules of conversation, such as starting, stopping and waiting for a turn. ◆ Help the child use communication for more than just simple requests. Talk about communicating feelings or opinions. ◆ Ask other children in the setting to be peer buddies and talk with the child.

Should I stop trying to make her talk and use an alternative form of communication?

While learning to talk is always important, it may not be possible for all children. For children with autism, what is most important is that they communicate with purpose. Usually, when a child is not using words or word-like noises to request items, doesn't comment about things or respond to questions, it is time to consider using an alternative way to communicate. Just because a child learns to use an alternative form of communication does not necessarily mean she will never learn to speak. It may mean that she needs a bridge or a way to help her as she learns to speak.

Friends use pictures to communicate.

An alternative communication system is generally a method of communication that does not involve speech. Some children who remain non verbal may ultimately use devices that speak for them. However, for most non verbal pre-school children, a more functional system will include either sign language or pictures. Even if the child is starting to use speech, sign language and/or pictures can be used to supplement her communication and facilitate comprehension and organisation. They can also reduce the frustration she feels when she is unable to let people in her world know what she wants. Remember, children with autism are predominantly strong visual learners and visual communication systems allow more understanding of the child's environment and facilitate expression.

Numerous studies have shown the use of alternative communication aides, like visual symbols, does not keep a child who may develop speech from talking. Rather, these studies show that communication supports help children, and enhance the ability of children who do develop spoken language to do so more effectively. It is important that everyone work together to understand and support consistently the communication system that is most beneficial to the individual child.

When and how is the best way to use sign language?

Sign language may serve as a method of helping a child with autism communicate with the people in his world. Unfortunately, sign language is not universal and many people don't know even basic signs. In addition, some children don't have the motor skills to make signs and therefore approximate the sign or make one up on their own. This too, can be effective, if everyone recognises

Approximated sign for 'more'

and understands the approximated signs. So, sign language can be a valuable tool that you can use to help children learn to communicate. If you and the child's family have decided to use basic signs with him, it is always a good idea to make a list of the signs, as he learns them, so others in his world will be able to communicate with him. Learning signs can become a game that all the children in your setting will enjoy.

Deciding which signs to teach first can be difficult. However, think about which three signs might help the child most in his environment. For example, the signs *want, more* and *all done* (finished) represent things that the child might use frequently throughout the day. (For more information about teaching sign language see page 98.) These three signs can be a useful starting place for children, as they communicate many of the basic things for a child, and can be used in a variety of settings, including snack, meals, play and so on. The table below includes pictures of some of the most commonly used signs.

Commonly used signs

Word	Sign	Word	Sign	Word	Sign
eat	tap twice	drink		more	

Remember, just because a child begins to use signs to communicate does not necessarily mean he will always use signs. But whether sign language is a bridge to using more traditional forms of communication or a method that the child will use throughout his life, it will enable him to let others know what he wants and needs.

How can a child with autism use pictures to communicate?

Pictures are clearly more universal than sign language. Anyone, including a child's peer, can see if he points to or touches a picture of a toy that means he would like to play with that toy. Handing a picture to a communication partner is one way that the child can interact with that

partner. Pictures are used in various ways to make communication boards and visual timetables, which can be combined to describe concepts, ideas and feelings. With pictures, photos and symbols a child can indicate a choice, a preference or answer a question.

The most widely recognised formal system of communication is the Picture Exchange System (PECS). In the PECS system, a child presents pictures to a partner or selects pictures from a board or portable notebook. The pictures are inexpensive and portable, allowing the child to use them in a variety of different situations. While pictures are an excellent tool for children with autism, using the official PECS system requires special training, as there is a very specific method to presenting each sequence of pictures.

Pictures and photographs are great teaching tools, are practical, and easy to use, and also provide the opportunity for the child to use the same set of pictures at home or in his community. When using a picture communication system you might want to use the following guidelines:

◆ Help children become aware of how pictures can be used. Display picture schedules and refer to them often throughout the day. Use them to explain the sequence of an activity. Whenever you introduce a new

word, hold up the picture. Many children in the early years setting may benefit from the added cues that pictures provide.

◆ The ultimate goal in using a picture system is to teach children to initiate communication. Once the child becomes more familiar with the pictures encourage him to use them to start a communication interaction.

◆ Build a list of commonly used pictures and practise with the child. Share these pictures with home and encourage all the child's family to use them, too.

◆ Expand the picture list slowly and ask questions that require the child to answer you by pointing to a picture.

◆ As the child becomes more comfortable with using the picture communication system, expand the pictures to include action pictures and pictures that can be used to tell you what and how the child is feeling.

What about electronic communication devices?

While there are a few electronic communication devices simple enough for a young child to learn to use, young children usually do not use electronic

Augmentative device helps a child communicate

communication devices. These devices are designed to provide a source of communication, specifically speech, but often they are too expensive or too complex for a young child to use.

Single message switches are sometimes used to help children as they begin to communicate. They are button type switches on which a single

Introduce games that encourage communication.

message has been recorded. The child is taught to push the button and the message is spoken. Unlike more expensive devices, this switch can be used with multiple children and is often a great tool when children are learning to let you know they need to go to the bathroom. A picture of a bathroom or a toilet can easily be taped or attached to the switch. Whenever any child needs to go, they just walk up to the switch and push the button. This device can be a great communication starter or a tool to use when you want to encourage participation. The message is easily changed and the device is easy to operate. The child's speech and language therapist will recommend and introduce the most appropriate device.

Communication is a lifelong learning skill that facilitates social relationships and helps the child relate to his environment. Regardless of how much or how little a child communicates, he will benefit from practitioners who understand the following:

◆ how to encourage interaction
◆ how he communicates best
◆ why he communicates
◆ how to model appropriate language.

A reason to communicate

These activities include requiring the child to request, protest and/or comment on what is going on. The more effectively you can engineer activities to encourage children to do these things, the greater the likelihood that the communication will become intentional.

What to do

1. To facilitate a request, place a desired object slightly out of the child's reach. Wait, and briefly pretend that you don't know what he wants. If the child makes any attempt to request the item (gesture, sign and so on), hand it to him and say, 'Oh, you wanted the _____.'
2. Another way to encourage the child to request an object is to place a desired item in a container that the child cannot open. He then must gesture, sign or indicate what he wants you to do.
3. To further encourage the child to tell you what he wants, pretend you don't know, and see if he will persist in trying to tell you or show you what he wants.
4. To encourage the child to protest, hand him the wrong item or object and look at him as if you don't know what he wants. Do not frustrate him. Try to encourage the rule that 'Nothing is free!' You must ask, gesture or sign to get what you want.
5. Deliberately say or do something in the daily routine that is wrong. Sometimes children with autism will feel a compulsion to correct your mistake. This can lead to a more functional use of language.

Helpful hints

◆ Tell others what you are doing, so they will know you are trying to get the child to communicate.
◆ Play a game with children – tell them ahead of time that you will be doing something wrong and they must be a detective and find out what it is.
◆ Model with all the children in your group that to get what they want, it will be a requirement that they request it in some way.

Three basic signs

Remember to work closely with all the adults who interact with the child so that they will use these signs consistently – thank you, more and done (finished).

What to do

1. Teaching basic signs is dependent on the teacher being familiar with the signs and making them correctly. The table below shows the correct way to make each of the three signs.
2. Remember that other children in your class may also benefit from using signs to communicate, so use the signs with the entire class.
3. Practise the signs before you begin to use them with the child.
4. Sign to yourself in the mirror. Once you are confident that you know the three basic signs, begin to use them in the class.
5. **Always say the word** as you sign.
6. Don't force a child to use the signs. Simply model each sign as you use it.
7. Praise the child for any attempt to imitate the sign.
8. After the child is familiar with the three basic signs, it is time to encourage her to use them. Encourage the child to let you know when she wants more and when she has finished.

Helpful hints

◆ Make learning the signs a game that all the children can play.
◆ Encourage all children in the setting to use the signs with the child.
◆ Send home details about what and why you are teaching the three basic signs. Parents who may be initially resistant to the use of sign language are often more open to the idea when they understand why you are doing it.

Three basic signs

More   Thank you   All done (finished)

What is it? Using pictures to identify objects

Although a child with autism may know some words, he may not understand that pictures are symbols representing real objects.

What to do

1. Select five pictures that you want to use with the child. Make sure the pictures clearly represent one specific item or activity.
2. Select pictures of objects that are functional for the child and easily accessible in the setting.
3. Start with pictures that you can use with real objects. For example, a cup, ball, book, paintbrush and so on.
4. Pick up the object and the picture. Hand the object to the child. If he will not take it, try to direct his attention to the object. Play at matching the object to the picture.
5. As you match objects and pictures point to the picture and say the word.
6. Start with one or two pictures and build up to five.
7. Remember that the purpose of this activity is to help the child make the connection between the picture and the object.

Helpful hints

- The child's attention span may be short, so keep this activity short.
- Review the pictures throughout the day – little and often works best.
- Try to make this activity fun.
- Don't forget to work with his parents and other caregivers, so that they are reinforcing at home what you are doing in your setting. The more often he sees the pictures, the easier it will be for him to use them.

Communication apron

To make communication pictures more readily accessible. Start off with only a few cards attached to the apron. More can be added later.

What to do

1. Make or use an existing apron. A plastic craft apron or a vinyl bib apron works best.
2. Attach sticky-back Velcro to the apron.
3. Attach Velcro to the back of each picture to be used.
4. Attach the pictures to the apron. This provides an opportunity for the child to use language.
5. Remove the pictures when you need them and replace them when you have finished.
6. An alternative is to use clear plastic pockets to store the cards. The plastic pockets hold cards and more than one card can be placed in each pocket.

Helpful hints

- Make sure the cards are large enough for the child to see.
- Move beyond things – use pictures that show an action or activity that the child will do.
- Use the cards as cues for other children who are having trouble with language concepts.

Guidelines for picture schedules and visual timetables

To help the child understand what will happen in the daily routine. Even after the child has learned the daily routine, the picture schedule may help him feel that the day is organised and predictable.

What to do

1. Decide how you want to display the schedule. Select a place that is easily accessible to the child. Remember to keep the schedule in the same location. You can have mini-picture schedule(s) displayed throughout the room, but there should always be one location for the main schedule or timetable.
2. Decide how you will post the schedule. Clear plastic holders work best. Try using a hanging shoe bag with clear plastic pockets or purchasing clear pockets with a sticky back. These can be found at most office supply stores.
3. Make sure the pictures are sturdy enough to handle frequently. Laminating, if possible, helps to preserve them.
4. The pictures must not be too small. The minimum size should be 5cm x 5cm.

Helpful hints

- Refer to the schedule often throughout the day and use it with all the children in the setting.
- Use the schedule to let the child know what will happen next.
- When the schedule is going to change, be sure to change the schedule cards as well.
- Make sure all the adults who work with the child use the schedule to help him know what will be happening.

Sing to me: using music to communicate

Often a child with autism will sing when she might not be as open to a conversation. Use familiar songs and rhymes to help make communication fun, and learn new vocabulary.

What to do

1. Choose simple songs with tunes the child recognises. Songs with repeating words often work best.
2. Sing about activities or things that the child enjoys.
3. Stress key words, concepts or vocabulary.
4. Don't be concerned if you can't sing well; it's the interaction that children find enjoyable.
5. Use the child's name first whenever possible.
6. Consider the following examples.

New foods

A song to encourage eating
(sung to the tune of 'Mary Had a Little Lamb')

Mark is eating peas today, peas today, peas today,
Mark is eating peas today, I am so glad.

Or
_____ (child's name) *is trying* _____ (name of new food) *today,* _____
(name of new food) *today,* _____ (name of new food) *today,* _____
(child's name) *is trying* _____ (name of new food) *today, I am so glad.*

Play with me!

A song to encourage playing together
(sung to the tune of 'Twinkle, Twinkle Little Star')

Won't you come and play with me?
We'll have fun, just wait and see.
First it's your turn, then it's mine.
We'll be friends all the time.
Won't you come and play with me?
Well have fun, just wait and see.

An action song

*A song to describe an action
(sung to the tune of
'Row, Row, Row Your Boat')*

*Terrance has a bright blue car.
It's his favourite toy.
He will roll it up and down.
Terrance has a blue car.*

My friend

*A song about how to treat others
(sung to the tune of
'Old MacDonald Had a Farm')*

*Tamika plays so well.
She is my friend.
She takes turns and shares her toys.
She is a friend.
She treats others very well.
She is a friend.
She helps put up all the toys.
She is a friend.*

7. Once the child has learned the song, leave out words and wait expectantly for the child to fill them in. She may use a word picture, sign or gesture to fill in the missing parts of the song.

Helpful hints

◆ Work with groups of two or three children.
◆ Sing in a pleasant tone, keeping in mind that loud noises can overwhelm a child with autism.

Puppets as talking partners

Children with autism will often talk with an inanimate object before they talk to another person. Encourage communication and enhance make-believe play through puppets.

What to do

1. To help the child get used to a puppet, introduce the puppet into a small group activity. For example, a mouse puppet could help the class with a simple rhyme like 'Hickory, Dickory, Dock'.
2. Talk for the puppet, using a funny animated voice.
3. Make the puppet nod, move its head, look over at the child and then look away.
4. Smile, so that the child will understand this is a game.
5. Ask the child if he would like to hold the puppet.
6. If the child uses a pretend voice, continue to encourage him to talk to others or talk to you and tell you what he is doing.

Helpful hints

◆ If the child responds well to the puppet, introduce additional puppets.
◆ Expand the activity by encouraging the child to use puppets with a friend.
◆ Make a puppet theatre from a cardboard box.

Communication notebooks: opportunities for interaction

Communication notebooks are great tools to use to encourage children with autism to express their feelings.

What to do

1. Help the child record her experiences in a way that she can use to talk about things she has done or places she has visited. Communication notebooks also make great conversation starters.
2. Photo albums with individual pockets for pictures make great holders for the child's pictures. Wallets with fold-out plastic photo holders can also be used to make great picture stories.
3. To begin, take a single experience that the child has had and see if she will point to some pictures that tell you about what she saw, felt or did.

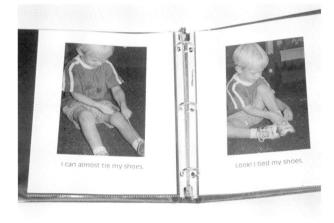

I can almost tie my shoes.

Look! I tied my shoes.

4. You can prompt the child by providing hints and picture cues.
5. Write a sentence to go with each page in the book.
6. Communication books also can be used to help the child express her emotions.
7. Encourage the child to share her communication book with others.

Helpful hints

◆ Encourage parents and other carers to make communication books. Knowing what the child enjoys at home can be very helpful when you are looking for conversation starters.

Key terms

Alternative communication system: A method of communication that does not involve speech.

Communication: An interaction between two or more people where information is exchanged.

Echolalia: The echoing and repetition of a phrase or word.

Electronic communication device: Sometimes called an augmentative communication device; a mechanical device that is designed to talk for the child, when it is activated either by a switch or by pressing a button.

Expressive communication: How the child inputs his message to the person receiving it. The method used to communicate with others.

Intentional communication: Communication that is on purpose or deliberate.

Language disorder: A deficit in using words or vocabulary. It can also involve how a child understands language and uses it in social settings.

Non-functional communication: Communication that lacks meaning or purpose.

Pragmatic language: Involves using language in a social setting. For example, knowing what is appropriate to say, when to say it and the general give-and-take nature of a friendly conversation.

Receptive communication: How the child receives messages or information from others.

CHAPTER 7

Inside their own worlds:
Encouraging children with autism to play

How does the play of children with autism differ from their peers?

For most children, play is a valuable and fun way to learn. It helps a child develop relationships with others, learn how to solve problems, express emotions, and use his imagination to create new experiences and explore the world around him. Play is the main vehicle through which children learn to get along with others and socialise; it is how a child experiments and solves problems in his world.

Play develops as the child begins to experience new activities and explore new environments. The solitary play of a toddler, with experience, develops into the interactive, reciprocal play of a pre-school age child.

While the stages of play have been described in many ways, most experts agree that typically developing children begin to explore their world by manipulating and experimenting with objects that interest them. Later, a child will become involved in a more functional type of play when she uses objects, such as placing a brick on top of another brick or putting a plastic spoon beside a bowl. As she develops cognitively, she may substitute one object for another, such as picking up a brick and pretending it's a camera. This will lead to imaginative play or pretend play.

New activities are fun.

In summary, play:

- is a fun and joyful experience
- requires that a child becomes an active participant
- is a voluntary experience that comes from within
- has no real agenda, except what the child wants it to be
- requires that a child learns to use symbols, such as when a cardboard box becomes a jet plane
- is the primary vehicle through which a child learns the rules of socialisation.

Play involves active participation.

When considering the major characteristics of autism, it is understandable why children with autism do not follow a typical pattern when they play. Because many children with autism become obsessed with objects in non-typical ways and do not socialise easily, their play is not as socially interactive as that of their peers. In addition, when we consider the communication issues and marked uninterest they often show for the world around them, it is no wonder that encouraging children with autism to play with others can be very challenging. Although children with autism may manipulate objects or engage in some form of experimental play, it is usually very different from that of their peers.

While they tend to be somewhat involved with materials and objects that involve the senses, children with autism often show a marked preference for only one type of play material. For example, Dan will build a road for his cars but he only uses square bricks and he only plays with red cars. Also, since children with autism are usually very literal, they do not always understand or show any desire to participate in symbolic or pretend play. In addition, make-believe and imaginative play, especially if it involves role-play or interaction with others, is very uncommon. For example, if asked to use sequence cards to retell the story of The Three Little Pigs,

Pretend or imaginative play

Jemima will gladly comply. However, when you ask several children to reenact the story, Jemima stares at the ceiling as if she does not understand what is being asked of her.

It is very difficult for the child with autism to understand the social relationships involved in playing successfully with others. Even if they are interested in such interaction, most children with autism do not know how

to engage themselves in a play activity with someone else. For this reason, they become even more socially isolated. While their peers are learning to build relationships in play groups and play activities, they are often left sitting alone, absorbed in a favourite toy. Jake, for example, enjoys making a collage out of bits of fabric, string and coloured paper. However, if you ask him to make a kite with a peer, he turns his back on you and walks away.

When we consider the communication issues and marked uninterest autistic children often show for the world around them, it is no wonder that encouraging them to play with others can be very challenging.

What can I do to encourage children to play?

Before you can encourage play, it is important to spend some time observing the child. Use the table on page 110 to make notes that will help you determine what interests the child most. Structuring play around his interests will greatly increase the chances of positive play interactions and will make him more likely to show an interest in what is going on.

How do I use what I have observed?

Once you have observed how a child plays and what she prefers to play with, it will be easier to plan activities that focus on her interests. Make sure the child has time to play with preferred objects and is not under stress to stop or share the toy until she is ready. Once the child has played with the preferred item for a few minutes, try to encourage her to try something new by putting the new toy beside her and walking away. Don't take away the preferred toy but, after a few minutes, return and ask if she would like to play with the new toy.

Another way to help the child to play with others is to ask a peer to help. However, it is important that you select a peer buddy who recognises that, while the child is different in the way she responds, she can still be fun to play with.

Play observations

Questions to ask	How does the child play?	Examples you observe
Does he prefer a toy or an object?	◆ What does he do with it? ◆ Does he play? ◆ Does he just watch while it moves? ◆ Does he just sit and stare at the object?	
What activity does he seem to repeat?	◆ How does he act when he is repeating the activity? ◆ Does it have more than one step? ◆ Will he let others engage in the activity with him?	
What resources does he use most often?	◆ Is his preference for colour or size? ◆ Does he prefer one texture over another? ◆ How does he respond when you introduce something new, such as a new toy?	
What does he do when he plays with an object or toy?	◆ Will he engage in multiple activities with the same toy? ◆ Will he let others share the toy with him? ◆ Does he play appropriately with the toy or does he just repeat a movement over and over?	
Does he have a collection or need to have an object with him when he plays?	◆ Will he put aside his desired object when something new is introduced?	
If he does engage in role-play, is there a theme he prefers?	◆ Does he use the same theme (pretending to be a doctor or a firefighter) every time he plays? ◆ Will he assign themes to other activities?	
Does he play with others? Who?	◆ If he does play with others, who does he play with most? ◆ Will he play with other children or just adults? ◆ How does he react when you bring over a new peer buddy to play with him?	

How do I select an appropriate peer buddy?

A peer buddy is a volunteer who agrees to play with the child for a given amount of time. Observe the other children in your class and try to determine who has interests that are similar to that of the child with autism. Next, look at individual characteristics. Which child might be more tolerant of a peer with autism? Who seems to be more patient with others? Who might be willing to play with the child, even if the child has rejected him as a friend in the past? For younger pre-schoolers, try to find a peer buddy who is four or five years old.

Peer buddies play together.

You may be able to identify a peer buddy immediately. At other times, you may have to be more creative and look outside your room for a first-time peer buddy. Maybe there is an older child in another group who can visit and be a peer buddy for a little while each day.

After you have selected the right peer buddy, you can begin helping the child with autism to play more effectively with others. The first step in this process is to look at the steps involved in learning to play with others.

How do I begin to teach this process?

Begin the process by interviewing the peer buddy and explaining that, over the next few days, you will need his help in playing with the child with autism. Remember to use the child's name, such as, 'Brandon, thank you so much for volunteering to be a peer buddy for Katie. Every day, I will tell you what I need you to do to help Katie learn to play.'

Next, invite the peer buddy to play beside the child for a few minutes. Do not encourage them to play together or to communicate. If that happens, great! But, at this point, you are trying to get the child with autism to accept someone else in her space. She must be willing to do this, before any type of cooperative play is possible. While you may not be able to teach a child with autism to make friends in the traditional sense, you may be able to orchestrate some situations that encourage positive interactions.

However, first, you must teach her to tolerate the presence of other children. Accepting the presence of others in her personal space is an important step in learning to play with peers.

After the peer buddy has played in the child's space for a few minutes, ask him to leave the area. It is important to introduce children with autism gradually to the presence of others. Later in the day (or the following day), ask the same peer to help again. This time, encourage him to play beside his friend with autism for a little longer. Continue this process for several days, before you start encouraging the children to share the same toys. After the child has learned to tolerate a peer and share the same toys, it is time gradually to introduce activities that will encourage the children to interact.

If the child is communicating with simple signs or using a communication device, teach the peer buddy and all the children in the setting to use that form of communication. Even if it is nothing more than making the sign for 'want' or 'more', it can be the first step to a positive play experience for both children.

Structure play around the interests of the child.

Ideas and activities for encouraging children to play

When trying to encourage a child with autism to play, keep the following points in mind:

◆ Focus on the interests of the child.
◆ Make interactions with others as natural as possible.
◆ Recognise that children with autism may have difficulty adjusting to new play situations and new resources.
◆ Explain activities that involve more than one step and provide picture cues to help the child know what to do next.
◆ Allow the child to leave an activity, if it becomes overwhelming.

- Respect the child's need to play alone; some pre-school children with autism aren't ready to play in large groups.
- Avoid upsetting the child; let her know ahead of time that it will soon be time to stop playing, so that she has time to accept that there will be a change.

General suggestions for teaching play strategies

Before selecting a strategy to help you encourage play, it is important to remember the following general suggestions:

- Introduce one new toy or activity at a time. Too much change can be overwhelming.
- If you are teaching the child to do something for the first time, break it down into a few simple steps.
- Show him each step. Then, ask him to repeat it after you.
- Start off with very short periods of structured play. Then, make the time longer as the child learns to tolerate the activity.
- Talk about the activity. Be animated and use a positive approach by saying such things as, 'Wow, I just love rolling the ball to you!' or, 'You built that tower really high, isn't this fun?'

Solitary play

- If the child is prone to a self-stimulatory activity, such as hand flapping or hitting himself, try to find an activity that requires him to use his hands in other ways.
- When teaching a new skill, use the child's name and tell him what will happen next.
- Next, show him or model the steps in the activity, and encourage the child to try the activity on his own.
- Make sure every play activity is fun and rewarding for the child. Remember, the main reason children play is because it is fun!

Give and take – learning reciprocity

Initially, this strategy involves just you and the child; later, it can be expanded to include other children. This strategy works best when the child is relaxed. It will help the child participate in a basic give-and-take game with another person.

What to do

1. Sit facing the child. You will need to sit close to her but respect her personal space. Later, as she learns what to do, you can move back.
2. Hold up the item you want to exchange (ball, car, doll and so on). Make sure the toy is in the child's line of vision. Smile and show lots of interest in the toy.
3. Use the child's name and the toy's name in a sentence. For example, 'Sarah, look, Miss Lynne has a doll.'
4. Repeat step 3 until the child glances at the doll. When she does, look at the doll and place it in her hand.
5. Identify the doll as the child's. For example, say, 'Sarah's doll,' pause, and see if the child will hold the doll.
6. Gently take the doll back, and say, 'Miss Lynne's doll'. Place your free hand on your chest and gently tap it a couple of times as a cue that says, 'mine'. Say, 'Mine'.
7. Repeat the process, using the same words each time. Remember to pause to give the child an opportunity to take the doll.
8. After a few times of taking the doll back, wait, and extend your hand, to see if the child will place the doll into your hand.

Helpful hints

- Be aware that it may take many tries before the child begins to hand you the item without your having to take it back.
- Once the child has become accustomed to the routine, try using other toys. This encourages the child to generalise what she has learned to other objects.
- After the child has become familiar with what to do, sit further and further away from her. When you are confident that she understands how to exchange a toy in a playful way, ask another peer to join in and try the activity with her.

It's my space – a strategy to encourage children to play side by side

To encourage children to tolerate the presence of other children in their play space and to encourage parallel playing.

What to do

1. Make sure the play area has clearly defined boundaries, such as shelves or an area rug.
2. Allow the child to spend time in the play area alone, before introducing another child into the area.
3. Place one or two toys nearby that the child enjoys playing with.
4. After he has played for a few minutes, put a few toys nearby that his peers enjoy playing with.
5. Ask one or more children to play in the same area as the child with autism, but instruct them to play with the toys you have put there for them. Use the child's name and say, '_____ is playing on his own right now. Would you like to play next to him?'

Accepting the presence of others is important.

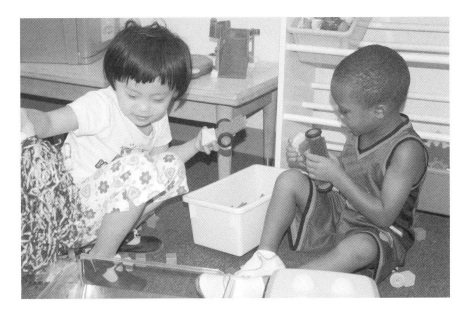

6. Select toys for peers that can easily be shared, if the two children decide to play together. Examples might include bricks, art supplies or toys with wheels, such as cars and lorries.

7. Don't interrupt the children while they are playing unless the child with autism becomes upset and reacts. When they have finished, gently and softly make a statement that lets him know you are pleased that he let his peer play beside him. For example, 'Michael, thank you for letting Laura play with you today.'

8. As the child begins to tolerate others in his play space, introduce more toys and more children to the play area.

Helpful hints

- ◆ A crowded, disorganised play area may be very confusing for the child, especially if he likes things neatly arranged in specific places.
- ◆ Be sure that you put the play resources in the same place on the same shelf every day, because routine is very important to children with autism.
- ◆ Visual drawings or picture cues make it easier for a child with autism to know where a specific toy is located.
- ◆ Some children function better when toys are placed in plastic containers rather than placed randomly on a shelf.

Feely bag game – what did you find?

To encourage natural curiosity and provide opportunities for structured interaction with peers.

What to do

1. Gather together a feely bag and four or five items from the room, such as a small ball, a piece of wool, a crayon, a rock, a plastic spoon, soft material or a cotton wool ball.
2. Explain that you are going to play a guessing game.
3. Tell the children that each child will have a turn to reach into the bag and guess what's inside. Be sure to put only one item in at a time.
4. Ask the first child to reach inside and feel the item. Let each child have a turn before anyone guesses what's inside.
5. Vary the game by asking the child to describe what's inside without naming it.
6. After the child has described what he feels, ask if anyone in the group wants to guess what's inside the bag.
7. Later, after the children are more familiar with the game, let one person be 'it'. The other children will close their eyes while 'it' goes around the room and selects a small item to place inside the bag. Then, the other children can open their eyes and reach inside to feel what is hidden there.

Helpful hints

- If a child is hesitant to be 'it', encourage him to choose a friend and they can be 'it' together.
- Only play the game for as long as the children are interested. Once they start to get tired, discontinue the game and go on to another activity.
- Remember that children with autism often do not like to touch certain textures. Use items that you know will be pleasant for the child with autism to touch and explore.

The basics of simple games – learning about rules

To help children understand basic social rules for playing in small groups or for playing with others.

What to do

1. Introduce group rules to a few children at the same time. Explain that these rules will be displayed with pictures so that everyone can see them when they are playing.
2. Limit the group rules to just a few, and decide ahead of time what your rules will be. For example, with three-year-olds, the following rules might be useful:
   ◆ Be nice to everyone.
   ◆ Be gentle with toys.
   For older children, expand the rules to include such things as:
   ◆ Ask for help.
   ◆ Put toys away when you have finished.
3. Once you have established group play rules, display them in the play area. Use pictures whenever possible.
4. Review the rules often and refer to them each day, before the children begin to play.
5. The first few times you introduce the rules, model each one for the children and ask them to follow the rule with you.
6. If a child forgets a rule, take her over to the rule list and go over just the rule that she forgot to use.
7. Make going over the rules part of the daily routine, so that children learn to expect it as something that is done before they enter the play area.

Helpful hints

◆ Make sure the rules are stated in a proactive and positive way.
◆ Refer to the pictures and explain clearly what each rule and each picture means.
◆ Be sure the rules are displayed at the child's eye level.

Same old, same old – introducing a new toy

Use this strategy when the child is relaxed and having fun. It is less effective when the child is over-stimulated by the environment or when he is tired.

What to do

1. Before the child becomes involved in the activity, place the new toy on a table and cover it loosely with a piece of cloth.
2. Tell the child that you have hidden something under the cloth on the table and you want to see if he can figure out what it is.
3. Sit down with the child in front of the hidden toy. Lightly touch the toy without removing the blanket. Make a comment, such as, 'Hmmm… this feels soft' or 'Listen, I think this toy makes a noise.'
4. Encourage the child to explore the toy without looking under the cloth.
5. Continue to explore the toy. Say things like, 'Do you think it's a _____?'
6. After a few minutes, ask the child to guess what is hidden under the cloth. Pause, and wait for him to answer.
7. Lift the cloth with the child and say, 'Oh look, it's a _____ (fill in the name of the toy).'

Helpful hints

◆ Children with autism are often hesitant to explore new toys. Think of creative ways to get their attention directed to the new toy.
◆ After you have uncovered the toy, ask the child to play with it or ask him to take it to the shelf where it belongs.
◆ Initially, use a toy that you know will interest the child. Later, you can try the same activity with a toy that will be less familiar to the child.

Scarf dance

This strategy works best in a small-group setting. It is also important to have plenty of space for the children to move around. Make sure the children know where the designated space for this activity is, such as on the carpet in a particular area of the room.

What to do

1. You will need scarves or brightly coloured material cut into long strips (crêpe paper streamers can also be used but they are less durable) and music that can be quickly stopped and restarted.
2. Smile and hold up your scarf. Tell the children you are going to play a game where they wave their scarves and move to the music.
3. Tell the children you will show them how to play the game. Play the music and gently move around, while waving your scarf in time to the music.
4. Hand each child a scarf and let him practise waving the scarf to music.
5. Tell the children that when the music stops, they must stop in place until the music starts again. Practise and model this step several times.
6. Initially, stop the music very soon after you start it. Later, wait longer before stopping the music.
7. Continue to model the game until the child with autism understands what to do. If he seems confused, stand next to him and gently guide him as the music plays.

Helpful hints

- Experiment with different types of music to see which one works best.
- A variation of this game is to use art supplies and encourage children to paint or draw to the music, stopping when the music stops.

May I play, too? Asking to join a game or activity

To teach the child a strategy to use when asking to join an activity or game. This strategy is most effective with children who are more able, such as children with Asperger's Syndrome.

What to do

1. Use this strategy when you want to teach the child appropriate ways to join in the activities or play of others.
2. Prepare four index cards, glue, pictures showing: walk, stop, listen (ears with cupped hand) and '?'. Glue one picture on each card. Then, lay the cards out in the following order: walk, stop, listen and '?'.
3. Tell the child that you are going to show him the steps to follow when he wants to join in a game or activity.
4. Go over each step and point to the card. For example, say, 'First, you walk up to where the other children are playing.' Point to the card showing 'walk'. 'Next, you stop and watch.' Point to the card with 'stop' on it. 'Then, you listen', and 'Last of all, you ask a question. You ask, "May I play, too?"'

5. Tell the child that you will practise each step with him. Go over each step several times, and model exactly what to do.

6. Ask several peers to help you demonstrate the rules for joining in a game. See if they will role-play what to do.

Helpful hints

♦ Although this strategy is designed for children with autism, it is a good social skill for all children to learn.

♦ Ask all the children in the class to use this procedure when they want to join in a game.

♦ To encourage the child with autism to try this strategy, set up a game that you know he will especially enjoy and see if you can prompt him to request to join the game.

♦ Ask others in the class to remember that he is practising a new skill and encourage them to let him join in, when he asks.

Time to stop – putting away toys and activities

To help the child stop playing when prompted and to help put away toys without getting angry or upset. This strategy is most effective if you give the child ample notice that it will soon be time to tidy up.

What to do

1. Find a small bell, buzzer or chime bar.
2. Announce that it will soon be time to clear up the toys. Tell the children that when they hear the bell ring twice, it means that it is almost time to tidy up.
2. After you ring the bell twice, wait approximately three to four minutes and ring the bell once again. Explain that this single ring means it is time to tidy up.
3. Teach the group the tidy up song, sung to the tune of 'Here We Go Round the Mulberry Bush'.

   This is way we tidy up our toys.
   Tidy our toys, tidy our toys.
   This is the way we tidy our toys.
   In Miss _____'s nursery (fill in the blank with your name).
4. Tell the children that after you ring the bell once, you will start to hum the song. When they hear you humming, they must stop and finish what they are doing.
5. Sing the song and encourage everyone to sing along as they pick up the toys.
6. Go over all the steps and practise what they have to do: two rings means a few more minutes to play, one ring means time to finish the activity and the song means tidy up time.

Helpful hints

- It may be necessary to review the steps several times before the child with autism sees this as part of the daily routine.
- Be sure to share this routine with others.
- If the child is still playing when you get through singing, walk over to the area where he is and gently begin humming or singing the song. Pick up a toy, put it away and ask him to help you tidy up.

Once upon a time...playing with props

To help the child participate in a play activity involving props.

What to do

1. Select the activity that you want to use, based on your observations of the child's preferences. Look around the setting for items that can be used in pretend play.

2. Explain to a few children (no more than three) that you will tell them a story and you want them to act it out. Demonstrate and model what you want the children to do. For example, if the story is about looking for a bear, show the child how to pretend she is looking for a bear.

3. Sometimes, it is easier for the child to role-play a familiar story, such as 'Goldilocks' or 'The Three Little Pigs.'

4. Encourage the group to make up a story and act it out.

5. Some children, particularly those with Asperger's Syndrome, might be more prone to act out a scene from a film or a familiar TV show. This is often a good starting point.

6. If necessary, introduce a prop and model for the child and show her exactly how to use it before encouraging her to begin interacting with peers.

Helpful hints

◆ Keep it simple.
◆ Experiment with different props and/or storylines to see which one works best.
◆ Later, as play becomes more advanced, encourage the children to make up their own imaginary stories.

Key terms

Imaginative play: Play activities that involve using imagination and creativity.

Parallel play: Play, where one child plays near or beside another child and may even share some of the same toys, but they do not play together in a reciprocal fashion.

Peer buddy: Someone who is assigned to interact and play with a child for a short time.

Personal space: The space in which someone feels comfortable – their comfort zone.

Pretend play: Make-believe play.

Reciprocal play: Direct play with a partner where the children interact with each other and take turns.

Socialisation: The ability to get along with others.

Solitary play: Playing alone or play that does not involve others.

Symbolic play: Using one object or toy to represent another, such as pretending a square brick is a camera or that a cardboard box is a jet plane.

CHAPTER 8

Building social skills:
Getting along with others

Playing with peers

Why are social skills important?

Pre-school is a time when children learn the fundamental skills necessary to get along with others. It is a time when they learn how to make friends, how to treat other people and how to interact socially. In pre-school, children learn to collaborate with other children. Most children with autism have considerable difficulty behaving appropriately in social situations. In fact, one of the defining characteristics of autism is an inability to see situations from someone else's point of view.

Children with autism don't develop social skills in the same way as their peers. While typically developing children learn social skills through observation and experience, children with autism struggle with social cues and have difficulty establishing lasting social relationships. In order to select a social skills strategy for a child, it is important to know about the stages of social development.

What are the stages of social development?

Social development depends on many factors. For example, contact with other children and the presence or absence of siblings in the home are contributing factors in a child's ability to interact socially. In general, social development occurs in conjunction with cognitive and emotional development. As a child matures, his social relationships will become more complex. The table on page 127 summarises the major characteristics in the social development of children aged two to five.

Major characteristics of social development

Approximate age of child	Primary social characteristics
Two years old	◆ Plays alone ◆ Is egocentric and self-absorbed ◆ Depends on adults for guidance ◆ May socialise to get something, but has little understanding of the feelings and needs of others
Three years old	◆ Begins to learn to take turns ◆ Begins to know the difference between girls and boys ◆ Enjoys simple group activities ◆ Likes to help with small chores ◆ Responds to adult approval or disapproval ◆ Has a rudimentary understanding of empathy and the point of view of others
Four years old	◆ Becomes very social and plays simple games with rules ◆ Selects a peer and might even play exclusively with that peer ◆ Understands more fully that others have feelings and needs ◆ Responds when someone else is unhappy or sad
Five years old	◆ Enjoys and takes pride in accomplishments ◆ Will play with friends and shows a distinct preference for specific friends ◆ Understands the abstract nature of social interactions ◆ Can usually tell the difference between a light-hearted remark and a remark that is serious ◆ Laughs and shows emotional responses freely

Which social skills should be learned first?

By definition, a socially competent child has developed strong interpersonal communication skills, knows how to form relationships with peers and understands the value of appropriately interacting with others.

Think about a child in your setting that you would characterise as popular. Perhaps this child is always invited to birthday parties or seems to be a natural group leader. What makes this child so popular? If you observe the child, you are likely to see that she is popular because she has learned how to make other children feel important, to recognise the preferences of others and to behave in socially acceptable ways. In other words, she has

Socially competent pre-schoolers take pride in their accomplishments.

All the characteristics of a socially competent child depend on his being able to use and understand language.

learned what it takes to be liked by others. Learning how to adapt to a social situation and behaving accordingly is a skill she will use throughout her life. Therefore, an important characteristic of the socially competent child is that she knows how to make adaptations to her own behaviour so that others will want to be her friend.

Another characteristic of the socially competent pre-schooler is that he is able to control his own behaviour. Studies have consistently shown that children are more likely to want to play with a child whom they perceive as having self-control. Generally, self-controlled children manage their anger and do not have violent outbursts. In addition, they are not aggressive towards themselves or others. Finally, socially competent pre-schoolers have self-confidence. As a result, they are not afraid to try new things or experiment with novel situations. Confident children enjoy things that challenge them and feel a sense of accomplishment when they succeed at a new task. When a peer doesn't want to play with him, a confident child either adjusts his behaviour so the peer will play with him, or he finds someone else who will. All the characteristics of a socially competent child depend on his being able to use and understand language.

Other children help social development.

With this in mind, consider a child with autism who does not know how to interact and read social cues, cannot control his behaviour, and lacks the confidence to enjoy new situations. Furthermore, the child probably has no idea how to interpret, much less understand, the preferences and feelings of others, and more than likely has a significant language delay. For these reasons, social skills training for children with autism is critically important.

How do I teach social skills to a child with autism?

Most children learn social skills through experience and observation. They watch how other children act and what other children do in social settings.

Then, based on their observations, they imitate the behaviour of others. For children with autism, it is not as easy as that. They often lack the ability to learn social skills through observation or to interpret social cues. While typically-developing children are likely to benefit from observing a social situation, a child with autism usually needs more. He must learn techniques that will help him respond appropriately in social settings. One technique that helps children with autism learn social skills is called the 'social story'.

What are social stories?

Social stories present appropriate social behaviours in the context of a story. Each story includes answers to questions that children with autism need to know in order to interact with others. In other words, a social story answers who, what, when, where and why questions about social interaction. In some senses, a social story can teach the child with autism to respond to others, even if he does not fully understand why he is doing so. By simply imitating in a real-life setting what happened in the story, the child begins to experience some semblance of social interaction with a peer.

Developing social skills through play

Social stories help the child with autism learn to predict how others might act in a social situation, by giving her a better understanding of the thoughts, feelings and points of view of other children. Social stories also help the child with autism learn more about what might be expected of her in such a setting. However, before deciding how to use social stories, it is important to observe the child and decide which of the three types of social impairment best applies.

What are the three types of social impairment?

The first type of social impairment is characterised by the socially avoidant child. This child may try to escape a social situation by having a tantrum, being aggressive towards others or hiding. Some children are socially avoidant because the environment has become too much for them – the

noise, smells, lights and overwhelming number of other children is more than they can stand. The only way they know how to react is to escape the situation altogether.

The second type of social impairment includes children who are **socially indifferent**. Although they may not avoid socialisation by withdrawing or getting upset, they do not actively attempt to interact with others. Children in this category are happier being alone and have considerable difficulty making and keeping friends. A socially indifferent child allows social interactions to go on around him while remaining passive and makes no attempt to join in the interaction.

Social awkwardness is the defining characteristic of the final type

Turning away from play

of social impairment. These children tend to be higher-functioning. For example, many children with Asperger's Syndrome fit into this group. While they will interact socially, their conversations seem to be focused on subjects of interest to them. They may talk about something they like but fail to respond when another child wants to change the subject or offer a comment. Socially awkward children do not understand the rules of polite conversation and can't grasp the concept of small talk. The general rule for children in this group is, 'If it's not about something that interests me – it's not worth talking about.' Socially awkward children probably benefit the most from the use of social stories.

How do I write a social story?

Once you have determined in which category of social impairment a child belongs, it is time to begin observing the child. General guidelines for observing the child include:

♦ Observe the child on multiple occasions.
♦ Watch the child in a variety of settings.
♦ Make careful notes about interests and preferences.
♦ Make a list of the children he plays with most often.
♦ Determine if there are certain activities, toys or people that upset him.

Before writing a social story, it's always a good idea to call a team meeting. Bring together the people who work with the child and his parents and ask them to comment on how they have observed him in social situations. Compare their observations with yours. Next, decide on what social skill you want to work on first. Remember, children with autism often have social difficulties because they cannot seem to understand what is expected of them. Let's look at some examples.

> *William, a child with Asperger's syndrome, likes football. He frequently puts on his football gloves, gets his ball and approaches a peer. William does not understand that the peer may be engaged in doing something else. Instead of asking the peer to play football with him, William throws the ball at the other child. When the peer turns away from William, he gets upset.*

An appropriate social story for William might include how to ask others to play with him.

> *Amanda, a child with autism, frequently screams when she wants to go to the computer activity. On one particular occasion, she found other children working collaboratively on the computer. Instead of asking if she might join in, she attempted to push another child out of the chair.*

Amanda would benefit from a social story that involves learning to ask others to let her have a turn or learning how to ask if she can join in a collaborative activity.

Once you have determined which social skill you want to focus on, it is time to start writing a social story. As you begin to write, keep in mind that social stories are:

> Remember, children with autism often have social difficulties because they cannot seem to understand what is expected of them.

◆ short
◆ written in first person
◆ usually in present tense
◆ designed to help the child learn how to act in a social situation.

Four types of sentences make up a social story: descriptive, perspective, directive and control. Descriptive sentences address the who, what, where and why of the social situation. Perspective sentences give information

about the thoughts, feelings and emotions of others. Directive sentences tell the child how he might respond to the situation. In other words, a directive sentence suggests a specific action on the part of the child that will enhance the social interaction.

Control sentences are more complex and are usually only used with high-functioning children. The control sentence is something that serves as a cue or hint to remind the child how to react in a social setting. Control sentences are generally not appropriate for pre-school children. When they are used with younger children, they must be short and easy to remember. For example, after learning about conversation, the child might remember to stop, look and listen: stop after he has spoken, look at the other person and listen to what the other person is saying.

There is a general acceptance that it is important that for each directive sentence, a ratio of at least three descriptive or perspective sentences be used. Later, as the child becomes more socially competent, stories can be written with no directive sentences. The child can learn to decide for himself how he should respond or react. It is also recommended that absolute statements be replaced with statements that are more flexible. For example, instead of writing, 'I will ask for a turn' or 'I can sit in a circle', the child might say, 'I will try to ask for a turn' or 'I will try to sit in a circle.'

Let's look at a social story written for William, the child who enjoys football. Remember, his problem is that he does not know how to ask other children to play football with him.

> *I like to play football. I have a new ball and goalie gloves. I want Tom to play with me. Tom is having fun playing with his cars. When I want Tom to play with me, I will tap him on the shoulder. I will say, 'Tom, would you play football with me?' I will try not to just throw the ball at Tom when I want him to play with me. I will try to learn to ask Tom to play football.*

Finally, let's look at a social story written for Amanda, who wants to join Lauren in an art activity but does not know how to ask.

> *I go to the art activity. Other children are playing there. Lauren is painting at the easel. I want to paint, too! I will try to wait until Lauren has finished. I will try to ask if I can paint at the easel with Lauren. If she says no, I will go to another activity.*

Hi! My name is _____.

To teach the child to introduce himself and say 'Hello' and 'Goodbye' to a new person.

What to do

1. Teach the child the process involved in meeting someone new:
   - Walk up to the person you want to meet.
   - Stand one arm-length away. (**Note:** Practise where to stand, as children with autism often have difficulty knowing how close or how far back to stand.)
   - Look at the person's face. Smile.
   - Say, 'Hi, my name is _____ (fill in the child's name).'
   - Wait!
   - Say, 'I like to _____ (fill in something the child likes to do).'
   - Wait!
   - Say, 'Bye.'
   - Wait! Walk away.
2. Go through each step, one at a time. Ask the child to do each step immediately after you model it for her.
3. Provide opportunities for the child to practise. Ask other children if they would like to pretend they are meeting someone new.
4. Review the steps often.
5. At first, the child may not be able to remember all the steps. If she forgets, remind her gently by saying, 'Next, you _____.'

Helpful hints

- After the child has practised several times in the one room, take her to another part of the setting and introduce her to someone she has not met.

Building social skills

Something good about me!

To teach the child to say something that he likes about himself. This strategy works best when the child is verbal or after the child has started using either signs or picture cards to communicate consistently.

What to do

1. Teach the class the following song.

   ME (sung to the tune of 'Mary Had a Little Lamb')
   I am very proud of me,
   Proud of me, proud of me.
   I am very proud of me
   Because I can _____ (fill in the blank)!

2. The first time you sing the song, fill in the blank yourself and add a skill. For example:

   I am very proud of me,
   Proud of me, proud of me.
   I am very proud of me
   Because I can hop! (Hop one time)

3. Sing the song several times, adding new verses each time.

4. After the children have sung the song several times, ask each child to tell you one thing they are proud of about themselves. After the child has said what he is proud of about himself, sing the song in a different way. For example, if Jack says he is proud of himself because he can throw a ball, you would sing:

   We are very proud of Jack,
   Proud of Jack, proud of Jack.
   We are very proud of Jack
   Because he can throw a ball!

Taking turns is important.

5. Repeat the activity with each child in the group, until everyone has had a turn. If the child with autism cannot think of anything to say, you may have to make a suggestion or ask his peers to help.

6. Try this song when a child is just learning a new skill as well. For example:

I am very proud of Nakisha,
Proud of Nakisha, proud of Nakisha.
I am very proud of Nakisha
Because she is learning to share!

Helpful hints

◆ Later, after the children have learned how to play the game and sing the song, see if they will play the game by saying something they are proud of about someone else.
◆ Share the song with the child's family so they can sing it, too.
◆ This is a great activity when you want to help the child build self-esteem and identify strengths.

Talk to me!

To help the child learn how to have a conversation with others.

What to do

1. Write a simple social story for a conversation. It might go something like this:

   I want to talk to _____ (fill in a child's name).
   I will walk up to _____ (fill in a child's name).
   I will say, 'Hi!'
   I will wait for him to say, 'Hi.'
   I will look at him and say, 'What are you doing?'
   I will wait for him to speak.
   I will say, 'That sounds like fun.'
   I will wait for him to speak.
   I will look at him.
   I will say, 'Bye!'

2. Ask the child with autism to say the name of or point to someone he would like to talk to. If he does not do so, then you point to someone and say, 'Let's talk to _____ (fill in the peer's name).'
3. Go over these steps with the child. Ask him to imitate each step as you read the social story. Review the steps often.
4. Ask a peer to help you practise this routine with the child.
5. Go through each step often. If the child does not wait or starts to walk away, remind him what to do next.
6. If the child is non verbal, adapt the sequence using picture cards.

Helpful hints

◆ Display cue cards in the room that show the steps in a conversation.

◆ Role-play with small groups of children.

Teaching Young Children with Autism

Telephone talk: following simple directions

To teach the child to follow a simple direction while interacting with a peer or an adult.

What to do

1. Find two paper cups, string or wool and adult scissors.
2. Using the scissors, make a small hole in the bottom of each cup (adult-only step).

   Put a piece of string or wool through each hole and tie a large knot.
3. Tell the child with autism you are going to play a game with him. Place one cup to your ear and hold it there. Ask the child to take the other cup. If the child is hesitant, ask a peer to help you demonstrate what to do.
4. Say something to the person on the other end of the 'phone', such as, 'Hello. Can you touch your nose?'
5. Continue to ask the person to do something simple, such as, 'Wave at me' or 'Turn around once.'
6. Remember that pre-school children are normally quite curious, so others may want to play, too.
7. After you have given a few simple directions, see if the child on the other end of the line will take turns to give you a command.

Helpful hints

◆ Tell the children that this is like a real phone in that one person receives a message and another person responds.
◆ Once the child is familiar with the game, try to get him to play it with his peers.
◆ As the child learns to follow one-step directions, add more information, such as two-step directions. For example, 'Touch your nose and then wave at me.'

Learning to say, 'Thank you!'

This strategy should be taught one-on-one. To use this strategy, the child must be able to say or sign, 'Thank you!'

What to do

1. Decide whether you are going to encourage the child to say, 'Thank you!' or say and sign, 'Thank you!' (You may decide to do both.)
2. If you are going to use the sign, demonstrate how to use it. The sign for 'Thank you' is made by touching your lips with the tips of the fingers of your right hand. Move your hand away from your face, palms upward. Smile.

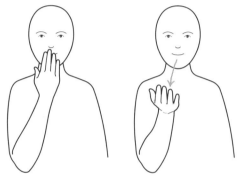

3. Tell the child that you are going to teach him what to do when someone does something for him. Explain that saying or signing, 'Thank you!' lets the other person know that you like what he did for you.
4. Recite the following jingle for the child:
   When you like what others do
   Smile at them (smile) *and say, 'Thank you!'*
5. Use the rhyme frequently with all of the children in the class.
6. Model saying and/or using the sign for 'Thank you' when anyone in the class does something for someone else.

Helpful hints

◆ Send a letter home telling the child's parents that you are working on saying, 'Thank you!' (Include a copy of the jingle for them to use at home.)
◆ Praise children when they say or sign, 'Thank you!'

Three breaths away (a strategy for calming down)

To learn a simple technique to help the child with autism calm himself so he won't get upset with others.

What to do

1. Tell the child you are going to show him something he can do when he is getting stressed by people or situations.
2. Tell him that it involves breathing. First say, 'I want you to breathe with me. We will take a big breath, hold it and then see if we can blow all the breath out.'
3. Practise together. Take a deep breath. Hold. Blow out all the air.
4. Next say, 'I will bring my hands together (place your hands in front of you as if you are going to clap).'
5. Then say, 'Now, I will put my hands down and take another breath.'
6. Repeat this process, until you have done it three times.
7. Say to the child, 'Next time you think you are getting upset, come and get me and we will breathe.'
8. Try to provide opportunities for the child to practise this technique.
9. Remember, if the child can focus on breathing before he gets too upset, the strategy has a much better chance of being successful.

Helpful hints

◆ It may take several attempts before the child understands what you are asking him to do.
◆ Don't give up – keep trying. Once the child learns to do this strategy, it can greatly reduce outbursts.
◆ Share the strategy with the child's parents and encourage them to practise it, too.

Building a sense of community with a job

This strategy works best when you have had time to observe the child and match him with a job that suits his needs and interests.

What to do

1. You will need a photo of each child placed on a display board with space underneath it to attach an object that represents the child's job for the week or month; pictures to represent each classroom task, such as a cloth, a brick, a sign that says 'milk', a book, a mat for use in group time, a plate.

2. Hold up objects that represent the classroom jobs. Tell the children that the jobs will change in _____ weeks or days, so that they know they will have the opportunity to change jobs. (If you prefer, have a picture that shows the job so the child can attach the picture to the space under his photo.)

3. Tell the children that if they are interested in that job they should raise their hands.

4. If more than one child volunteers and it is a job that two children can do, such as tidying up the construction area or handing out plates for snack time, then let the children share the job.

5. You may be surprised to find that the child with autism will raise his hand to volunteer for a job. If he does not, then you could assign him a job by saying, 'Thomas, you will be the milk delivery person this week. That means you will give everyone milk during snack time.'

6. If necessary, assign another child to help the child with autism.

7. After you fill each job, ask the child to go and attach the object that represents the job under their photo.

8. After each child has been assigned a task, model for the child with autism exactly what he is to do in his job. Break each step down and teach him one step at a time.

9. The first time the child performs his job, it may be necessary to act as a job coach and assist him.

Helpful hints

◆ This is a great activity for when you want to build a sense of community and make the child feel part of the setting.

◆ If a child cannot do a complete job independently, let him participate partially. For example, if his job is to hand out milk at snack time and he cannot do it, perhaps he can walk beside a peer and hold the straws while the peer gives the milk out.

◆ Use the whole concept of jobs to demonstrate good behaviour on a job, such as saying or signing, 'Thank you!'

◆ Because resistance to a change in routine is very common in children with autism, you may want to change his job less often than you do the other children.

◆ The more a child does something, the more confident he will become and the more he will enjoy being successful at the task.

The Incey Wincey Spider! (Learning to try again!)

To encourage the child with autism to try something again that she has struggled with in the past.

What to do

1. Create cutouts of spiders (use craft foam, card or felt) and magnetic tape.

2. Make refrigerator magnets. Attach a small strip of magnetic tape to each cutout spider. On each spider, write, 'I got the Incey Wincey Spider Award today for _____ (fill in the blank with what the child tried to do).'

3. Sing the song, 'The Incey Wincey Spider' with the children. Do the hand actions, too.

4. Ask the children if they know what the song is about. Talk about how the spider tried again and again to go up the spout.

5. Tell the children it doesn't matter whether the spider ever made it up the spout or not. What is important is that he tried.

6. Ask them if they think it was hard for the spider to climb up the spout. Talk about things that they find hard to do.

7. Hold up one of the Incey Wincey Spider cutouts. Read what it says. Tell the children that you are going to be watching them, and if you see someone who keeps trying, you are going to give that person an Incey Wincey Spider Award.

8. Talk about how important it is to keep trying and not to give up. Sing the song again.

9. Place the Incey Wincey Spider Award magnet in the child's take-home folder with a note to his family. Encourage them to place the magnet on the fridge at home and to praise the child for his effort at trying something new.

Helpful hints

- When you see the child try something that is hard, be sure to praise him.
- Remind the child that the spider never gave up.
- When the child gets an Incey Wincey Spider to wear, write down what he did on the spider. It will help others to talk to the child about their achievements.

Key terms

Control sentence: Control sentences are used in social stories and serve as a cue or hint to remind the child how to react in a social setting.

Descriptive sentence: Type of sentence used in social stories to address the who, what, where and why of the social situation.

Directive sentence: Type of sentence used in social stories to tell the child how to respond to a situation. It suggests a specific action on the part of the child that will enhance the social interaction.

Egocentric: Self-absorbed, believing the world revolves around them.

Perspective sentence: Type of sentence used in social stories to provide information about the thoughts, feelings and emotions of others.

Social story: A strategy where stories are used to help children with autism learn social interaction skills in the context of a story.

Socially avoidant: A type of social impairment characterised by a child who tries to escape social situations.

Socially awkward: A type of social impairment characterised by a child who does not understand the give-and-take nature of a social interaction.

Socially competent: By definition, a socially competent child has developed strong interpersonal communication skills, knows how to form relationships with peers and understands the value of appropriately interacting with others.

Socially indifferent: A type of social impairment characterised by a child who is indifferent to social situations.

CHAPTER 9

Lights! Camera! Action!
Sensory integration and autism

Select activities that encourage the child to use his motor skills.

What exactly is sensory integration?

Sensory integration (SI) is a process that occurs in the brain. It allows us to take in information through our senses, organise it, and respond accordingly to the environment. It is also the process that allows us to filter out any unneeded sensory information. For example, when you walk into a noisy cafeteria, it is sensory integration that gives you the ability to filter out the surrounding noise so that you can enjoy your lunch or chat with a friend. When asked to name their senses, most people think only of the obvious ones: sight, hearing, touch, taste and smell. Nevertheless, there are two 'hidden' senses that are just as important.

What are the hidden senses?

The hidden senses include the 'vestibular' sense and the 'proprioceptive' sense. Both of these senses play an important role in helping the child integrate all the information he receives from the environment.

The vestibular sense provides information through the inner ear about balance, movement and gravity. In other words, it is the vestibular sense that lets a child know how to position his head and body in relation to the earth.

The vestibular sense affects:

◆ the sense of balance or equilibrium
◆ the way the eyes and hands work together (eye–hand coordination)
◆ the ability to move both sides of the body together
◆ movement of the head.

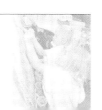

The proprioceptive system receives information from joints, muscles and ligaments. It is this sense that lets a child know where his body parts are and what they are doing. For example, information provided for a child by this system might tell her how far it is for her to reach to pick up a toy and how much pressure is comfortable or uncomfortable to parts of her body.

These two senses work together to help regulate the nervous system and build the foundation for purposeful movement. When a child cannot regulate the information he receives from his senses, he may have a sensory integration disorder.

Using touch is important.

What do we mean by a sensory integration disorder?

Almost 50 years ago, an occupational therapist named Jean Ayres described a condition that resulted from an insufficient process in the brain. She used the term 'sensory integration dysfunction' (SI dysfunction) to describe a child who is unable to analyse and respond appropriately to the information he receives from his senses. A child with SI dysfunction has problems adapting to the everyday sensations that others take for granted. Today, the terms sensory integration and sensory integration disorder and sensory issues are used. Regardless of which term is used, many experts believe that a sensory integration problem is the root cause of many of the behaviours commonly seen in children with autism.

Do you mean that children with autism see or hear differently?

Children with autism can hear and see just like other children. What many are unable to do, however, is to take the information that they see, hear, taste, feel or touch and translate it into a meaningful response. In other words, what may seem like normal lighting to you might seem like

dazzling spotlights to the child with autism. The normal chatter heard in a room where children work and play can be unbearably loud to a child with sensory integration issues. Children with autism are often unable to regulate or modulate the input they receive through their senses. Because such information is sometimes so overpowering, they will have problems learning and interacting in their environments.

What may seem like normal classroom lighting to you might seem like megawatt spotlights to the child with autism.

Remember, most children enjoy activities that involve movement, such as dancing to a favourite tune or jumping up and down. In addition, pre-school children thrive on opportunities to touch new things and enjoy using their hands for activities such as making a mountain from clay or painting with their fingers. Pre-school children can sit on a carpet square and listen to a story, play in the sand tray and smell a fresh flower with delight. However, for a child with autism who has a sensory integration disorder, these activities can be frightening, confusing and overwhelming.

How will I know if a child has a sensory integration disorder?

You will know it by observation, through information you receive from others, and by educating yourself about ways to recognise it. A few of the most common red flags that a child has a sensory integration disorder include unusual responses to touch, adverse responses to moving and being moved, a lack of tolerance for noise and light, and an unwillingness to taste or try new foods.

The following are a few examples of how a child with sensory integration disorder might respond to everyday early years situations:

Scott walks into your room and looks around. He immediately goes to the sink in the back of the room and turns on the tap. He watches as the water comes out. He places his hands in the water. He fails to notice anything except the running water.

It is time to get ready for lunch and you have called Maria, by

name, several times. Instead of responding, she continues to stare at the rotating blades of the ceiling fan as they whirl around. A few minutes earlier, when another child was sharpening a pencil, Maria responded by looking around frantically. Yet now she does not seem to hear you call her name.

Adam arrives in your room and you start to say, 'Good morning.' Instead of speaking or looking at you, he begins to tell you that the bookshelf in the corner has been moved since yesterday. He can talk about nothing but his concern over the bookcase being out of place.

Mi-Ling does not enjoy circle time. She will not sit still while you read. She stands up and begins to spin around and around in front of her chair.

These are all examples of how a child with autism who has a sensory integration disorder might respond. Rather than being over-sensitive (**hyper-sensitive**) to sensory stimulation, as are the children in the examples above, some children with autism are actually under-sensitive (**hypo-sensitive**). They seem to be in another sphere where they can't see, hear, feel or touch anything at all. Children who are under-sensitive to sensory information are at a greater risk of getting hurt. Because they don't often respond to sound, they may walk in front of a car. A child who is under-sensitive might pick up a hot object or fall down a flight of stairs without ever making a sound.

Movement activities are fun sensory experiences.

How do I know if a child is over-sensitive or under-sensitive?

The table on page 148 serves as a guide to the degree of response a child might have with respect to the senses. However, the child's occupational therapist is your best source of information about sensory integration disorder.

Sense responses

Sense	Over-sensitive	Under-sensitive
Vision (sight)	◆ Covers his eyes when the lights are too bright ◆ Overwhelmed by too many colours and items in the room ◆ Rubs his eyes or squints his eyes frequently	◆ Does not respond to light ◆ Holds items close to her face as if she can't see them ◆ Stares at flickering fluorescent lights
Sound	◆ Covers his ears ◆ Responds to sounds other children ignore ◆ Will act as if he can't hear when you call his name, but then responds when a child drops a toy ◆ Yells with fingers in his ears	◆ Speaks loudly ◆ Turns the volume up on the TV or computer ◆ Sings loudly ◆ Always plays with toys that make loud noises
Smell	◆ Holds her nose at common smells ◆ Sniffs the air or sniffs other people	◆ Ignores bad smells ◆ May sniff people or toys
Touch (tactile)	◆ Gets upset when someone touches him ◆ Very sensitive to textures and materials ◆ Opposed to getting dirty or touching certain toys ◆ Scratches at his skin or is startled when something touches him	◆ Bumps into people ◆ Chews on items frequently ◆ Unaware of temperature changes ◆ Seemingly unable to tell when she is in pain or hurt ◆ Does not cry when she falls down
Taste	◆ Gags when he eats ◆ Only eats food of a certain texture ◆ Sensitive to hot or cold foods	◆ Wants only spicy food ◆ Adds lots of pepper or salt to her food ◆ Licks objects or toys
Movement	◆ Does not like to move, dance, climb or hop ◆ Sways ◆ Seems to walk 'off-balance'	◆ Does not get dizzy when he whirls or turns around ◆ Loves to move fast ◆ In constant motion ◆ Rocks back and forth ◆ Moves his body all the time

What can I do to help a child with sensory integration disorder?

Children with sensory integration disorders sometimes respond well to items that enable them to calm down so that they can better organise all the input they receive through their senses. Some examples of such calming objects (calmers) and organisers include: things to chew on (chewies), toys that vibrate, weighted vests, soft things that

Getting under a blanket is a sensory game.

they can squeeze, beanbag chairs or therapy balls to sit on and stretchy material such as latex that they can use to make a body cocoon.

The most common calmers and organisers include:

Chewies: For a child with issues relating to touch, chewing on something soft can be very relaxing. Chewies can be purchased from companies that specialise in sensory integration materials.

Children with sensory integration disorders sometimes respond well to items that enable them to calm down so that they can better organise all the input they receive through their senses.

Vibrating toys: Vibration can be very calming to the proprioceptive system. Examples of vibrating items might include pens, toothbrushes, toys, pillows and mobile phones.

Weighted objects: A weighted object might be used to help a child who has difficulty with balance or with his proprioceptive system. A weighted vest, back pack or blanket can help the child feel more grounded and less concerned about his sense of movement. Deep pressure helps children feel calm.

Oral motor activities: Designed to help the child with issues related to his mouth and to touch. Blowing bubbles, eating crunchy foods, biting on a flannel and blowing a cotton wool ball across the table with a straw can help the child satisfy her need for oral stimulation and movement.

What can I do to make sure that a child with autism does not go into sensory overload?

One of the most important things you can do is to make sure that the light in the setting is not too bright. Fluorescent lights can be especially distracting

Activity with pressure and space

for children with autism. Look for ways you can use indirect lighting (lamps, for example), or at the very least, non-fluorescent overhead lights.

Regulate the noise so that it is not so loud that a child is unable to function. Watch for signs that the child is being overwhelmed by the noise in the room; for example, if he begins to look around the room nervously, begins fidgeting or covers his ears with his hands. Provide a quiet place for the child to go to desensitise and get away from the noise.

There are, of course, times when noise is unavoidable. For example, when the teacher says it is time to go outside, the children in the class put away their toys. This is can be a noisy few minutes.

Jake begins to scream, because the noise resulting from everyone rushing around to put things in bins, on shelves and in containers is just too loud for him. To alleviate the problem, Jake could go to the toilet and get ready for outside play while the class puts away the toys. The trip to the toilet serves two important purposes: first, it alleviates Jake's screaming because he is no longer experiencing the loud room; and second, it gives Jake a predictable toilet schedule.

> **AVOID SENSORY OVERLOAD**
>
> ◆ Use indirect lighting or non-fluorescent overhead lighting.
> ◆ Be aware of the effect of the noise level in the setting.
> ◆ Use textures to calm children.
> ◆ Use mild, natural scents in the classroom.

Consider the texture of the materials in the activities and include items with textures that you know the child might enjoy. If experience has shown that he seems to do better with soft textures, provide a softer surface for him to play on, such as a mat or rug. Using something as simple as a foam hair curler as a pencil grip can make all the difference in whether a child learns to write or avoids it all together. A child who can never sit on a carpet square during circle time might be more content sitting on a beanbag chair or balancing himself on a large therapy ball.

Be aware of the smells in your setting. To you, the sweet smell of rose scented air fresher might be pleasing and enhance your room. However, it could interfere with the ability of a child with autism to learn. If you use scents in the classroom, use natural ones, and then only after you have determined that the child with autism can tolerate them. For example, try peppermint, lavender or vanilla, instead of sweet flowery scents.

Snuggle blanket

To create a snuggle blanket that will help a child with tactile sensitivity and issues with her proprioceptive system to calm down when things become overwhelming.

What to do

1. Find three to four metres of Lycra or other stretchy material.
2. Select a colour and pattern that you know the child will enjoy.
3. Sew a small 1cm to 1.5cm hem around the material to keep it from fraying.
4. Hang the blanket in a location that is convenient for the child. She can retrieve the blanket and wrap up in it for comfort whenever she feels overwhelmed.

Helpful hints

◆ Traditionally, stretchy frabric works best. However, you might experiment with other types of fabric, perhaps fake fur or a very smooth shiny material.
◆ Make several blankets and encourage other children to use them as well.

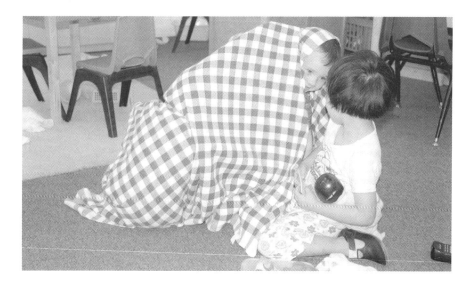

Monster shapes

To encourage children to explore new shapes and textures. To experiment with a variety of shapes and colours.

What to do

1. Gather together materials with different textures, such as cardboard of varying thickness, craft foam squares, cloth of various colours and textures; construction paper; scissors; glue or glue sticks; uncut poster board.
2. Pre-cut shapes in a variety of colours, shapes and sizes.
3. Give each child a piece of large paper or poster board and a glue stick. (Children with autism will often use a glue stick when they will not use glue.)
4. Tell the children that you are going to create monsters from the various shapes on the table. It's fine if you want to model for them how to put shapes together to make the monster, but avoid making a pattern for them to copy.
5. The child may want to arrange his monster shapes on the paper before he starts to glue. After the child has glued his monster together, allow time for it to dry.
6. Return to the project later and add details with crayons or markers. Encourage the child to give his monster a name.

Helpful hints

- Display the monsters round the room.
- Use a washing line to hang all the monsters on using wooden pegs.

Make and shake

To encourage children to use their listening skills and to help develop attention skills.

What to do

1. Gather enough plastic containers so each child has one. Pringles™ cans work well.
2. Give the children scraps of brightly coloured paper or cloth, and encourage each child to decorate their container with crayons. For a child who will not or cannot decorate the outside of her container, an alternative is to encourage her to decorate paper, and cover her container with the decorated paper. For a child who is extremely sensitive to touch, try covering her container with soft, fur-like material or velvet.
3. Once the children have decorated their containers, take them to a table where you have set up bowls of various materials, including coloured aquarium gravel, uncooked rice, sunflower seeds, sand and dried beans.
4. Using the scoop provided, each child fills her container with one or more items.
5. When a child has filled her container with a combination she likes, ask her to close the lid and shake it gently. It is easier to add more now rather than trying to add more after you have glued the container shut.
6. Glue the lids to the containers and allow them to dry.
7. When the containers are dry, the children take turns shaking each others' containers.
8. Ask the children to guess what is making the noise in each one.

Helpful hint

◆ If you want to tone down the container's noise level put some soft fabric at the base and top of the container and the sound will be softer.

Make a fidgety-widgety toy

Learning to regulate her own behaviour is a very important step in the child's overall social and emotional development and will help the child remain calm.

What to do

1. The fidgety-widgety is simply a toy that the child squeezes when she wants to remain calm.
2. To make it, fill a deflated helium-quality balloon or a sturdy, resealable plastic bag with flour, sand or oatmeal.
3. Tie the end of the balloon or seal the plastic bag. If using a plastic bag, place it inside another plastic bag for added safety.
4. Cover the balloon or bag with soft cloth and seal the end.
5. Introduce the toy to the child and demonstrate how to squeeze it. Encourage the child to squeeze it, too.
6. Place the toy in a place that is easily accessible to the child.
7. When the ingredients in the fidgety-widgety begin to wear out, it can be replaced easily.

Helpful hints

- Experiment with various textures, colours and sizes.
- Make the toy small enough that the child can hold it in her hand.
- The fidgety-widgety is not designed to be a chew toy and should only be used in the presence of an adult.

Step with me

To help the child practise and control his balance.

What to do

1. Trace each child's footprint. Use as many different colours of paper as possible.
2. Cut out each footprint and attach it to the floor. Place the footprints at various distances apart.
3. Invite the children to step on the footprints.
4. For added variety, if a child steps outside the footprints, he can go to the end of the line and start again.

Helpful hints

◆ Try doing the activity to music.
◆ After the children have got used to human footprints, vary the game by adding paw prints or dinosaur prints.

Cocoon

To help the child relax by applying deep pressure to the body. Children who don't like to be touched are often very comfortable with this activity.

What to do

1. You will need a foam-type mat, lightweight sleeping bag or rubber gym mat; a large, sturdy beach ball or therapy ball.
2. Play a game with the child. Using deep even pressure, press the ball up and down the child's body. Say something like, 'We're pretending you are a worm. We need to get you ready for your cocoon.'
3. Say to the child, 'Tell me when you want me to stop.' Pause and see if the child responds.
4. Next say, 'Are you ready to get in your cocoon?' Gently, but firmly, roll the child up in the mat or sleeping bag. This is best accomplished by putting one hand on the child's shoulder and the other hand on his hip or leg.
5. Rock the child back and forth gently a few times.
6. When you have determined that the child is ready to stop, say, 'Now we are going to pretend you are a butterfly.'
7. Gently, unroll the child by grasping the edge of the mat. If possible, encourage the child to unroll himself while you hold firmly to the mat.

Helpful hints

- This activity can be a fun and relaxing way to help the child cope with sensory overload.
- If the child does not want his whole body in the cocoon, try just his torso, hands or feet.
- Safety is always the most important consideration. Never cover a child's head when rolling him up in the mat, and always remember that this activity requires adult supervision.

Standing-up push-ups!

To help the child keep calm and move from one activity to another.

What to do

1. Select a large, solid structure in the room or playground. A wall or a permanent structure works best.
2. Walk up to the wall and say, 'I'm going to do some standing-up push-ups.'
3. Place your hands against the wall and count to 10.
4. Use varying amounts of pressure and smile at the child while you push against the wall.
5. Invite the child to join you in a standing-up push-up.
6. To encourage interaction, invite other peers to join in the fun.

Helpful hints

- Remember, this activity requires adult supervision.
- Encourage the child to try this with other parts of his body as well, such as his hips, back or using his feet while lying down.

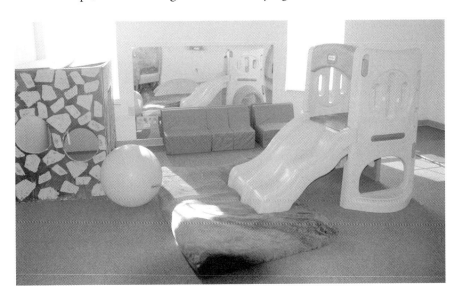

Key terms

Hyper-sensitive: Overly sensitive to sensory stimulation.

Hypo-sensitive: Under-sensitive to sensory stimulation.

Proprioceptive sense: The sense that receives information from joints, muscles and ligaments, providing information about where parts of the body are and what they are doing.

Sensory integration: The process by which the brain takes in and interprets information about the body and its surroundings.

Vestibular sense: The sense that provides information through the inner ear about balance, movement (inner ear) and gravity.

CHAPTER 10

We're all in this together!
Teaming up with families

What can I do to understand a family's perspective?

Make every child feel part of the classroom community.

Unless you have a child with disabilities, you can never truly understand the perspective of parents who do. You can be very supportive and try to appreciate how parents might feel, but you can never really know the day-to-day realities of living with and caring for a child with disabilities. Remember every parent's experience will be unique to them.

For parents of a child with autism, their child is not just 'an autistic child'. He or she is special, and is a valued member of their family. Helen, the mother of Nathan, a child with autism, puts it this way:

> 'When Nathan was created, there was a microscopic change, which occurred randomly in nature. We don't know why it happened and we didn't cause it to happen...we've always tried to do our best with him, even if it was not what his therapists thought we should be doing. Please remember, Nathan is valued by his family...he is a joy and a gift. In fact, when he was almost a year old, we discovered the name Nathan means "Gift from God".'

When working with parents, it's best to appreciate that parents of a child with a disability are doing the best they can with the resources they have at that given time.

As an early years professional, your job is to help every child in your care to become part of the group. You know from experience that all

Involve everyone who works with the child in a team meeting.

children have strengths and challenges. Some children just happen to have more challenges than others. Parents often agree that the one thing that a key person can do to understand their perspective is to be respectful of their opinions and treat them as valued contributors. When you first meet with them, parents are usually aware that they have a child who is not like other children. They have probably seen more than one specialist and scoured the Internet searching for information about autism. A few may be lucky enough to be involved in parent support groups. Regardless of how much they already know, parents are always seeking more explanations and answers about what they can do to help their child. Help parents by making sure they know about resources that may be available to them.

Resources may include:

◆ access to specialists such as occupational therapists or speech and language therapists
◆ information about local support groups for families
◆ suggestions about where they might go to obtain adaptive equipment or specialised materials for their child
◆ names of community organisations that provide support for children with disabilities
◆ government resources that they may be entitled to receive
◆ organisations that specialise in autism, such as the National Autistic Society (www.autism.org.uk).

Special needs literature is full of information about the value of enabling and empowering families to become self-advocates. When you enable a family, you give them the tools they need to make informed decisions; when you empower them, you show them how to use those tools. What this means is that you become an avenue through which parents learn to use the resources and tools available to them in order to advocate for what is in the best interest of their child.

Teachers can help parents by making sure they know about resources that may be available to them.

It is important to note that, at various times in the life of a child with autism, his family experiences a cycle of grief and loss that is not unlike what is experienced when an immediate family member dies. Determining where a parent is functioning within that cycle at the time the child enters your classroom provides a better understanding of that parent's point of view.

What is the cycle of grief and loss?

The grieving process that a family experiences when they discover their child has a disability or disorder has been compared to the grieving process that is associated with the death of a close relative. This process includes shock, denial, anger, despair and ultimately, acceptance.

Parents of children with disabilities never forget about their initial shock at being told their child has a disability. Articles written by parents of children with disabilities relate the circumstances under which they received the news. In the past, such news was often delivered in a clinical setting with little regard for the feelings of the family, where questions about the prognosis for the child or how to best treat the child were often answered with medical jargon that parents did not understand. Today, many parents report that their initial diagnosis was given in a very loving and supportive manner by a caring professional who answered their questions with information they could use. In many cases, from the moment a diagnosis is received, parents have access to counsellors and health care professionals who help them cope with the diagnosis.

No matter how gently a parent is told about their child's disability, it is always a shock. Unlike most childhood illnesses that are cured with medication or therapy, families must face a situation that is on-going. Brian, the father of a child with autism, related the following: 'We walked outside after hearing that Billy has autism, and people were walking to their cars, the sun was shining and the world looked so normal. How could it all look the same? Our lives would never be the same again!'

After the initial shock begins to wear off, many parents move into a phase known as denial. During this phase, the family is finding out that their perfect child, their gift, has something wrong with him. This is especially difficult for families of children with autism, because often that diagnosis takes months or years to obtain. While one or both parents may feel that something is not

quite right with their child, it is not until a diagnosis is confirmed that they begin to face the reality of life with a child with disabilities.

It is not uncommon at this point for a parent who has been given a diagnosis to seek out multiple opinions. In fact, one or both parents may begin to shop for a cure. That means that they search for anyone or anything that might give them answers.

During the next phase, parents begin to experience strong emotions, such as anger and despair, and may feel the need to blame someone for the child's disabilities. It is not uncommon to experience a feeling that we are in this alone and a sometimes overwhelming anger at the stressful situation or circumstance in which they find themselves. It is during this phase that strain is placed on relationships and families may begin to face great difficulty and begin to fall apart. One spouse may blame the other for not spending more time at home or not accepting enough responsibility for the child. Self-blame is also common, as a parent (usually the mother) feels that she did something wrong during pregnancy that caused the child to have autism. Brandy, the mother of a six-year-old with autism, says, 'I keep going over and over the things I did when I was pregnant. I painted the baby's room, I had a stomach bug… Did any of these things cause Lee's autism? Did I cause him to be this way?'

Ultimately, most families come to accept the disability as being a part of who the child is and learn to appreciate the child for what he can do rather than what he can't do. Yet, as the child reaches various milestones in his life (starting school, reaching puberty and so on), families may revisit one or part of the cycle again. Regardless of where parents are functioning within the cycle of grief and loss, or what might be taking place at home, the best you can do is help the child to have a positive experience in your setting.

How do I let parents know I need their help?

As soon as you discover that you will have a child with autism in your setting, begin to communicate with his family. From the very first moment, when you meet them, use language that shows how you want them to be part of a team whose sole purpose is to plan for what is best for their child.

For example:

◆ Use words like 'we' and 'us' instead of 'me' and 'you'.
◆ Talk about their child's strengths and challenges.

- Ask them what they think, and then respect what they say.
- Use the child's name when you talk about him.
- Ask about the family's priorities. What would they like to see him accomplish?
- Always look for ways to help make all interactions with families a positive experience for both you and the family.

Treat parents as team members.

What can I do to make family interactions positive?

Although there are many types of families from various circumstances and with different issues, interactions with them can be positive and successful. To facilitate good interactions, it is important to do the following throughout the process:

- Plan ahead.
- Develop rapport by being respectful and attentive to what families say.
- Foster a sense of trust.
- Communicate frequently.
- Acknowledge and value input when it is given.

Planning ahead means that you schedule meetings in advance and at a time that is convenient for the family. This helps relieve their added stress of taking time off work, finding a babysitter or in some cases finding someone to bring them to the meeting. Keep meetings short, and try to avoid lengthy discussions about everything the child is *not* doing. If possible, write an agenda for the meeting and allow a set amount of time for each team member to give input. If parents know the purpose of the meeting ahead of time, they can come better prepared.

Be sure to start the meeting by telling the parent at least one positive thing about their child. It will not only set the tone for the meeting but it lets parents know that you are there for more than just telling them about problems with their child. Review the role they play in their child's programme.

The relationship that you build with the family depends on the rapport that you are able to establish. By respecting the needs and desires of the family, you are indicating that you value their input. Even though you may

A family lending library

have a difference of opinion about some aspect of the child's development, you can still share information with each other openly and honestly. Once you have established rapport with a child's family, it will be easier to discuss his needs and make plans to address those needs. Rapport leads to relationships, and relationships help build trust.

Before parents will trust you, they must be able to see that you are worthy of their trust. They want to know that you are concerned about their child's well-being and development and will take the steps necessary to create a positive environment for their child. It does not come easily or quickly. Once a level of trust is established, you are well on your way to being able to make decisions that are in the best interests of the child. Again, the purpose of this book is to help better prepare you for this.

Communicate with parents often and in a variety of ways. Communication provides an on-going association with them, as well as strengthening their confidence regarding their child's experience and progress. A communication notebook that is sent home regularly with the child can be a great way for you to tell parents what is going on in your setting or parents to tell you what is going on at home. Imagine how much easier it is, if you know ahead of time that the child did not sleep well the night before, or that he is anxious because one of his parents is going on a long business trip. It is always important to use a team approach and strive to make family interactions positive.

It is always important to use a team approach and strive to make family interactions positive.

Key terms

Adaptive equipment: Equipment that has been modified or changed so a person with special needs can use it more effectively.

Cycle of grief and loss: The cycle experienced when someone dies. This process includes shock, denial, anger, despair and ultimately, acceptance.

Occupational therapist: A specialist who helps the child learn to perform daily tasks required to be independent.

Speech and language therapist: A specialist who helps the child in the areas of speech, language and/or communication.

Glossary of terms

Adaptive equipment: Equipment which has been modified or changed so that a person with special needs can use it more effectively.

Aggression: Behaviour that is harmful to others, such as biting, hitting, slapping, kicking, pinching or pulling hair.

Alternative communication system: A method of communication that does not involve speech.

Anecdotal record: Ongoing notes made by the practitioner concerning a child's behaviour or performance of a task.

Approximation: An inexact representation of a skill or a word that is still close enough to be useful.

Attend: To pay attention to or to concentrate.

Augmentative forms of communication: An alternative way to communicate, such as a device that speaks for the child.

Autism: A complex developmental disability that typically appears during the first three years of life. To be diagnosed with autism, a person must demonstrate either delayed or atypical behaviours in at least one of three categories: interaction, communication or behaviour.

Autism Spectrum Disorder (ASD): Autism Spectrum Disorder (ASD) is a broad term which includes the classical form of autism as well as several related disabilities that share many of the same characteristics including difficulty with communication, socialisation and behaviour. It is called spectrum because autism and autism-related characteristics range from very mild to very severe.

Challenging behaviour: A problem behaviour defined as any action where the child deliberately hurts himself, injures others and/or causes damage to his environment.

Communication: An interaction between two or more people where information is exchanged.

Communicative replacement: A form of communication or a message that the child gives to you that replaces the behaviour.

Compulsive: Behaviours the child performs repeatedly that will be stopped and begun again, if a certain step is not performed exactly the same way every time.

Control sentence: Control sentences are used in social stories and serve as a cue or hint, to remind the child how to react in a social setting.

Cue: A hint that is a word, gesture or phrase.

Cycle of grief and loss: The cycle experienced when someone dies. This process includes shock, denial, anger, despair and ultimately, acceptance.

Descriptive sentence: Type of sentence used in social stories to address the who, what, where and why of the social situation.

Developmentally appropriate practices: Activities and educational experiences that match the child's age and stage of development.

Directive sentence: Type of sentence used in social stories to tell the child how to respond to a situation. It suggests a specific action on the part of the child that will enhance the social interaction.

Echolalia: The echoing and repetition of a phrase or word.

Egocentric: Self-absorbed, believing the world revolves around them.

Electronic communication device: Sometimes called an augmentative communication device; a mechanical device that is designed to talk for the child, when it is activated either by a switch or by pressing a button.

Expressive communication: How the child inputs his message to the person receiving it. The method used to communicate with others.

Food preferences: When the child will only eat certain foods. Some food preferences are preferential, in that while they prefer one food to another, the child will also eat non-preferred foods. Sometimes they are more absolute, in that the child will only eat certain foods to the exclusion of all others.

Form: The way a child behaves.

Function: The reason why something happens.

Functional assessment: An evaluation designed to determine the relationship between events in a child's environment and the occurrence of challenging behaviours.

Functional skills: Everyday skills that the child will use to be more independent, sometimes called self-help or independent living skills. Functional skills are the skills a child will use throughout his life such as brushing his teeth, going to the toilet and taking a bath.

Generalisation: Being able to perform the same task, skill or activity in a variety of settings or with a variety of people and/or different objects.

Hyper-sensitive: Overly sensitive to something. The state of being overly stimulated by the environment.

Hypo-sensitive: Under-sensitive to sensory stimulation.

Imaginative play: Play activities that involve using imagination.

Individual Education Plan (IEP): A personalised plan for a child designed by a team including the child's parents which outlines the educational goals and objectives for the child over a period of time.

Intentional communication: Communication that is on purpose or deliberate.

Language disorder: A deficit in using words or vocabulary. It can also involve how a child understands language and uses it in social settings.

Learned helplessness: When a child learns how to be helpless because he never has the opportunity to do anything for himself; instead, everything is done for him.

Life skills: Self-help skills, such as going to the toilet or washing hands.

Maladaptive behaviour: A behaviour that is not common in most children or one that is so severe that it interferes with learning.

Natural consequence: The logical result of an action.

Non-functional communication: Communication that lacks meaning or purpose.

Obsession: A strong inclination towards something to the point of excluding everything else, such as collecting spoons or watching the blades of a rotating ceiling fan.

Occupational therapist: A specialist who helps the child learn to perform daily tasks required to be independent.

Parallel play: Play, where one child plays near or beside another child and may even share some of the same toys, but they do not play together in a reciprocal fashion.

Peer buddy: Someone who is assigned to interact and play with a child for a given period of time.

People-first language: Referring to the person, and then the disability.

Perceptive communication: How the child receives messages or information from others.

Personal space: The space in which someone feels comfortable: their comfort zone.

Perspective sentence: Type of sentence used in social stories to provide information about the thoughts, feelings and emotions of others.

Picture apron: An apron worn by the teacher with pictures depicting the day's schedule.

Picture schedule: A series of pictures showing what is supposed to occur within an area or time-frame.

Portfolio: A collection of the child's best work across a specific period. The portfolio is not intended to represent all the child's work; it should showcase a child's best efforts across specific domains.

Pragmatic language: Involves using language in a social setting. For example, knowing what is appropriate to say, when to say it, and the general give and take nature of a friendly conversation.

Pretend play: Make-believe play.

Proactive: A procedure or action that happens before a problem occurs and is designed to prevent the problem or behaviour from occurring.

Proprioceptive sense: The sense that receives information from joints, muscles and ligaments, and provides information about where parts of the body are and what they are doing.

Reciprocal play: Direct play with a partner where the children interact with each other.

Ritual: A pattern or way of doing something that is not logical, such as only walking on the floor instead of carpet or having to arrange food in a certain order before it can be eaten.

Ritualistic: Following a set pattern or routine without variation.

Self-injurious behaviour: Something a child does to hurt herself in an effort to get out of a situation or an environment that is overwhelming, such as hitting or biting herself.

Sensory integration disorder (SI disorder): An inability to filter or screen out sensory-related input.

Setting event: Conditions that occur at the same time a challenging behaviour occurs.

Social story: A strategy in which stories are used to help children with autism learn social interaction skills in the context of a story.

Socialisation: The ability to get along with others.

Socially avoidant: A type of social impairment characterised by a child who tries to escape social situations.

Socially awkward: A type of social impairment characterised by a child who does not understand the give and take nature of a social interaction.

Socially competent: By definition, a socially competent child has developed strong interpersonal communication skills, knows how to form relationships with peers and understands the value of appropriately interacting with others.

Socially indifferent: A type of social impairment characterised by a child who is indifferent to social situations.

Solitary play: Playing alone or play that does not involve others.

Speech and language therapist: A specialist who helps the child in the areas of speech, language and communication.

Stereotypic behaviour: A behaviour that is carried out repeatedly and involves either movement of the child's body or movement of an object, such as repetitive hand flapping or saying the same phrase repeatedly.

Symbolic play: Using one object or toy to represent another, such as pretending a square brick is a camera or that a cardboard box is a jet plane.

Talking stick: A sealed, decorated tube with items inside that make interesting sounds.

Tantrum: Anger beyond what is normally seen in children, such as falling to the floor and screaming or throwing their bodies on the ground.

Task analysis: The breaking down of a skill into steps; step-by-step guide.

Transition: Moving from one activity or area in the setting to another.

Typically developing: A child who is developing at a rate similar to his peers; a term often used to describe a child without disabilities.

Vestibular sense: The sense that provides information through the inner ear about balance, movement and gravity.

Index

absolute statements 132
accessing community resources 50
action-reaction cycles 70
adaptive
    behaviours 14
    equipment 160, 164
advocates 160
aggressive 10, 22, 29, 128, 129
'All about me'
    book 39, 42–43
    notice board 42
American Psychological Association 7
anecdotal records 28–29, 30
anxiety/anxious 14, 21, 32, 69
anxiety attack see panic attack
approximation 57, 68
Asperger, Hans 7
Asperger's Syndrome 13–14, 121, 124, 130,
    131
attachments to/interaction with items/
    objects 20, 29, 31, 46, 69
attention deficit hyperactivity disorder
    14
attention, getting 18
autism
    assessment of a child with 27–29
    characteristics of, summary 29
    definition of 7–8
    diagnosis of 7, 8, 14, 161
    jargon related to 11
    myths about 10–11
    prevalence of 8
    spectrum 5, 6, 9, 16, 83
    treatment of 6, 8
Autism Spectrum Disorder (ASD)
    name, reasons for 9
    types of 12–14

backward chaining see reverse chaining
balance 144, 155
behaviour
    adapting 128
    atypical 7, 10, 17
    challenging 69–70, 81
        dealing with 70
    communicating through 22–24, 35
    control 15, 128
    form of 70, 71, 81
    function of 70–74, 81
        determining 71–73
    learning, interfering with 17
    maladaptive 17–18, 23, 24, 29, 30
    management 5
    ritualistic 14, 17, 18
    self-injurious 17, 18, 19, 70
    stereotypical 7, 8, 17, 18–19, 29, 30,
        79
        definition of 18
        way of communicating 18
    strategies 22
beta-endorphins 18, 30
biting 18, 19, 22, 23
blame 162
books that teach a lesson 44
brain
    and beta-endorphins 18, 30
    and serotonin 15, 21
    pathways in 15
breathing 139
brightness see lighting
bullying 35

calm 18, 154, 157
calmers 149
calming down 139

change
    reaction to/difficulties with 13, 26
    resistance to 59
Checklist for Autism in Toddlers (CHAT)
    14
checklists 14, 28
chewies 149
child care 8
children
    making feel part of the group 34–35
    preferences of 9, 37, 39
    strengths of 9, 12, 31, 35, 135, 160,
        162
    typically developing 9, 39
    visiting at home 31
circle time 51, 74
cognitive development 107, 127
communication 7, 8
    alternative forms of 92, 106
    apron 40, 100
    aspects of 82
    augmentative forms of 24, 30
    content 82
    definition of 82
    devices 24, 30, 95–96, 106, 112
    difficulties/problems 10, 13, 17, 29
    egocentric stage 88, 91, 127, 143
    emerging stage 89, 91
    expressive 86, 106
    form 82
    function 82
    helping a child 87–90
    intentional 86, 97, 106
    non-functional 83–84, 106
    non verbal 23–24, 29, 35, 43, 46, 48, 63,
        83, 92, 136
    notebooks 105
    pictures 24, 35, 94–95, 99, 100
    reason to 97
    receptive 86, 106
    reciprocal stage 89–90, 91
    requesting stage 88–89, 91
    skills 5, 43, 127
    stages of 88–91

    through behaviour 22–24, 35
    with family, initial 162–163
communicative replacement 74, 81
community, building a sense of 140–141
compulsive behaviour/rituals 21, 30
confidence 128
consistency 34–35, 73
continuum of spectrum 9
control 14, 21
    sentences 131, 132, 143
coordination difficulties 13
crossing the road 67
cues 23, 30, 105, 112, 116, 126, 128, 129, 136
cycle of grief and loss 161–162, 164

dance 120
decision-making 15
depression 13
descriptive sentences 131, 132, 143
development
    delayed 14
    gaps in 10
developmentally appropriate practices 16
directions, following simple 137
directive sentences 131, 132, 143
dressing 52, 62
DSM-IV-TR 7, 12
dyslexia 14

early
    diagnosis 14
    intervention 5, 14, 24
early years specialists 8
eating see food
echolalia 11, 16, 29, 84–85, 87, 106
education, planning 9, 15
egocentric 88, 91, 127, 143
emotional development 127
emotions, describing 80
environment
    arranging 32–33
    changes to 21, 23
    natural 54
    proactive 29, 72–73

environmental stimulation 21
equilibrium *see* balance
eye contact 24
eye–hand coordination 144

families
    decision-making role 15
    enabling/empowering 160
    involvement 54, 58, 67, 135, 162–163
    meeting 163
    perspective, understanding 159–161
    positive relationship with 8
    questions to ask 31–32, 36–37
    also see parents/carers
feeling cards 80
feelings, expressing 20
first-then cards 77
flexible statements 132
food 5, 17, 18, 26, 29, 52, 63–65, 74, 87,
        102, 146, 148
Free and Appropriate Public Education
        (FAPE) 16
friends, helping to make 36, 43, 45
frustration 18, 22, 31, 69, 84, 85
functional
    assessment 71–74, 81
    skills 50, 68

gender, autism in 10
generalisation 26, 30, 54
goals 16, 24, 28, 32, 59, 90–91
greeting children with autism 40–41
gross motor skills 87
group size 72, 112

hand
    flapping 8, 18, 29, 69, 79, 113
    wringing 7, 79
head banging 19
hidden senses 144–145
hitting 10, 18, 19, 22, 27, 29, 70, 71, 113
home–school connection 54
hygiene, personal 50
hyper-sensitivity 53, 68, 147–148, 158

hypo-sensitivity 147–148, 158

illness 17, 19, 26–27, 72
imagination, impairment of 7
impairments, triad of 7
independent 35, 59, 66, 141
Individual Education Plan (IEP) 16, 32
individual needs 12
injure 20, 69
intelligence 13
interaction 7, 24, 29, 46, 69, 73, 85–86, 90,
        95, 102, 108–109, 112, 126, 127, 128,
        129, 130, 137, 146, 157, 163–164
International Classification of Diseases 7
intervention programmes 12, 15

Kanner, Leo 7
kicking 8, 22

language
    clear 54
    delay 83, 128
    development 18
    difficulties 9–10, 17
    disorders 82–83, 106
    pragmatic 83, 106
learned helplessness 35, 49
learning difficulties 14, 25
life skills 17, 30
lighting 5, 17, 18, 23, 24, 34, 63, 64, 72, 130,
        145–146, 148, 149–150
literal 51, 90, 108

Makaton sign 57, 63
maladaptive behaviour 17–18, 23, 24, 29, 30
mealtimes *see* food
medical problems/issues 17, 26–27, 39, 61
medication 27
meeting people, practising 45, 133
modelling steps/activities 56, 59, 62, 96, 97,
        113, 118, 120, 133, 141
monotone 13
mornings, starting 40–41
moving, averse to 146, 148

multi-disciplinary team 14, 27–28
music 34, 40, 64, 67, 76, 77, 102–103, 120,
    123, 134–135, 155

National Autistic Society 12, 13, 160
natural consequence 70, 81
non verbal 23–24, 29, 35, 43, 46, 48, 63, 83,
    92, 136
notes, making 28–29, 30, 37, 58

observation 28, 109–110, 129, 130, 131, 146
obsessions 10, 14, 17, 18, 20, 26, 29, 30, 108
occupational therapists 147, 160, 164
oral motor activities 149
overload 5
over-sensitive *see* hyper-sensitivity
over-stimulation 18

paediatricians 14
panic attack 69
parenting 10
parents/carers
    assuring 39
    meeting 36–37, 131, 163
    working with 15, 24, 99
    also see families
Pathological Demand Annoyance 13, 14
peer buddy 38, 91, 109–112, 125
peers
    conversations with 89
    interacting with 90
    relationships with, developing 17
    socially rejecting children with autism
        73
peg, directing to 41
people-first language 37, 49
personal space 112, 125; *also see* play space
perspective sentences 131–132, 143
Pervasive Developmental Delay (PDD) 12
Pervasive Developmental Disorder Not
        Otherwise Specified (PDDNOS) 14
picture
    apron 49
    cards 62, 66, 100, 134, 136

communication systems 24, 35, 94–95,
    99, 100
schedules 32, 33–34, 38, 40, 49, 56, 58,
    63, 78, 94, 101
Picture Exchange System (PECS) 94
pinching 19, 22
planning for a child with autism 8, 9, 34–35
play 5, 9, 20, 91, 93, 94, 102, 104, 107–125,
    127
    asking to join 121–122
    encouraging 109, 111–113
    imaginative 107, 108, 125
    observation 109–110
    parallel 115, 125
    pretend 107, 108, 113, 124, 125
    reciprocal 107, 125
    solitary 107, 113, 125
    space 111, 115–116; *also see* personal
        space
    stages of 107
    symbolic 108, 125
    teaching strategies 113
portfolios 28, 30
positive 36, 164
Positron Emission Technology (PET) 15
praise 59, 62, 70, 77, 138, 142, 143
proactive 22, 29, 72–73, 81, 118
professionals, working together and with
        families 15
prompt cards 45
proprioceptive sense 144, 145, 149, 158
props, playing with 124
psychologists 14
puppets 75, 104

questions to ask about a child 31–32, 36–37
quiet area/place 19–20, 32–33, 150

records 28–29
redirect 70, 76
relationships
    social 7, 10, 17
    with families 8; *also see* families
    with peers 127

repetitive/repeated 5, 9, 18, 19, 20, 21, 27, 30, 70, 84, 86, 88, 89, 90
research 8, 15
resources 50, 73, 160
responding to greetings 40
reverse chaining 62, 68
reward 75
rituals 18, 21, 29, 30, 69
rocking 5, 7, 18, 19, 148
role-play 64, 67, 110, 122, 124, 136
routines
    adjusting to 41
    changes to 21, 72, 78, 141
    helping with 51
    importance of 50
    planning 63
    setting up/establishing 33–34, 58, 66, 101, 114
    simple, list of 52
rules 73, 118

schedules 32, 33–34, 38, 40, 49, 56, 58, 63, 78, 94, 101
school, visiting 31
scratching 19
screaming 8, 69, 71, 131, 150
self-care skills 52
self-esteem 135
self-expression 909
self-help
    behaviours 14
    skills 8, 17, 50–68
        definition of 50
        grouping of 52
        importance of 50–51
self-injurious behaviours 19, 30, 70
self-stimulatory activities 113
sensory
    input/stimuli, responses/sensitivity to 10, 15, 17, 25, 33
    integration (SI) 25, 144–158
        definition of 144, 158
    integration disorder/dysfunction (SI dysfunction) 25, 30, 145

overload 20, 21, 149–150, 156
sequence cards 53, 54, 66, 108
serotonin 15, 21
services 13, 14
setting events 71–72, 81
sickness see illness; medical problems/ issues
signals, use of 23, 75
sign language 92, 93–94, 138
signs 24, 35, 57, 63, 92, 93–94, 97, 98, 112, 134, 138
    teaching 98
single message switches 96
skills
    emerging 28
    functional 50, 68
    listening 153
    problem-solving 25–26
    self-help 8, 17, 50–68
    social 8, 14, 24, 73, 126–143
    teaching, how to 51–52, 113
smells, issues with/responses to 5, 17, 18, 23, 25, 38, 61, 130, 148, 150
social
    communication, impairment of 7
    development, stages of 126–127
    impairment, types of 129–130
    interaction 7, 13, 24, 29, 69, 73, 108– 109, 126, 127, 128, 129, 130
    isolation 69
    relationships, impairment of/ difficulties with 7, 10, 17, 108–109, 126
    skills 8, 14, 24, 73, 126–143
        importance of 126
        teaching 129–132
    stories 129–132, 136, 143
socialisation 74, 107, 125
socially
    avoidant 129–130, 143
    awkward 130, 143
    competent 127–128, 132, 143
    indifferent 130, 143
songs see music

sounds, responses/sensitivity to 18, 21, 24, 146, 148, 150
snuggle blanket 151
special education teachers 8
specialists 8
spectrum 5, 6, 9, 16, 83
speech and language
    intervention 5
    therapists/therapy 8, 11, 14, 31, 86, 96, 160, 164
squeezing 19
step families 42
stimulation 18
stress 20, 22, 37, 72, 74
structure 34–35, 72
symbols 24, 80, 92, 94
system overload 5

tactile sensitivity 11, 58, 79, 117, 146, 148, 150, 151, 156
talking stick 47, 49
tantrums 10, 17, 18, 21–23, 27, 29, 30, 35, 69, 73–74, 129
task analysis 53, 54, 62, 68
teaching new skills/tasks
    how to 51–52, 129–132
    planning 53–54
teeth, brushing 21, 50, 51, 52, 54, 55–56
textures, exploring new 152
thank you, learning to say 138, 141
themes, exploring 44
time-out area 20
toileting 50, 52, 57–61, 96, 150

tolerance, helping 47
toys 9, 20, 21, 31, 46, 72, 77, 109, 110, 113, 114, 115, 116, 118, 119, 123, 130, 149, 150, 154
    new 119
    putting away 123
    vibrating 149
training 8, 24, 94, 128
    in social skills 24, 128
transitions 5, 32, 34, 49
treatments 6, 8
triad of impairments 7, 13
trying again 142–143
tuning out 18, 19
typically developing children 9

under-sensitive see hypo-sensitivity
under-stimulated 18
unique 5, 10, 12
unwell see illness

values, exploring 44
verbalise 91
vestibular sense 144, 158
visiting 31
vocabulary
    deficit in using 82
    selecting/using 53, 55, 58
vocal tone, difficulties with 13

washing hands 21, 52, 66
waiting, practising 77
weighted objects 149

The Cleverness of Boys

Lynn Broadbent, Ros Bayley and Sally Featherstone

Is it time we stopped seeing boys as losers, with later development and a consequent certainty of failing in the current curriculum?

The differences between boys and girls, in development and attitude to learning, are well documented, and a formalised early curriculum emphasizes these differences. The abilities of most girls to meet goals for learning at an earlier age may result in a tendency to focus on trying to teach boys to learn like girls, instead of recognizing their unique gifts and abilities. If we are to help boys to become strong, competent learners from an early age, we must resist the temptation to feel sorry for them. We must dispel the myths about 'under-achievement', challenge stereotypical views of gender, and recognise the strengths and abilities of boys.

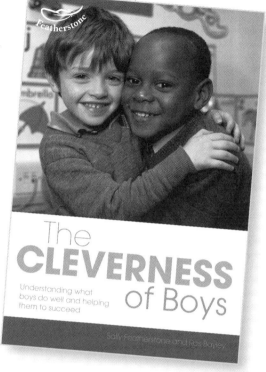

This book explores what boys are good at, and how early years practitioners and teachers can help young boys to become more resilient and successful in the early years, at school and in their future lives.

£17.99   ISBN 978-1-408114-68-1

To see the full range of Featherstone books visit www.acblack.com/featherstone